STRANGERS: THE UNLOVED, THE LOVED, THE LOST, AND THE LONELY.

Dr. S.R.G. Brush

PALMETTO
P U B L I S H I N G
Charleston, SC
www.PalmettoPublishing.com

The Unloved, the Loved, the Lost, and the Lonely
Copyright © 2024 by Dr. S.R.G.Brush
Cover illustration by Jordon Rifenberg
All rights reserved
No portion of this book may be reproduced, stored in a retrieval system, or transmitted in any form by any means–electronic, mechanical, photocopy, recording, or other–except for brief quotations in printed reviews, without prior permission of the author.
First Edition
Hardcover ISBN: 9798822958708
Paperback ISBN: 9798822958715
eBook ISBN: 9798822958722

TABLE OF CONTENTS

DEDICATION ix
PREFACE xiii
CHAPTER 1: *Introduction* 1
CHAPTER 2: *Just Like Any Other Kid* 11
CHAPTER 3: *Horsshit.* 16
CHAPTER 4: *The Police Report* 19
CHAPTER 5: *Meeting Wingnut in Her Early Days* 33
CHAPTER 6: *Simple Thoughts of the Author* 48
CHAPTER 7: *Digression to My Childhood* 50
CHAPTER 8: *Meeting Up with Horsshit* 57
CHAPTER 9: *Almost Coming Home* 63
CHAPTER 10: *Hopping Trains, Traveling Light, and Searching for Max* 66
CHAPTER 11: *Arriving in Amarillo* 73
CHAPTER 12: *Song of Stonie and Max* 81
CHAPTER 13: *Manitou Springs, Colorado* 88
CHAPTER 14: *Cali...forn...i...a* 92
CHAPTER 15: *July in the Slabs - One Way Ticket to India* 95
CHAPTER 16: *Missouri Bound for a Moment... ThenOff Again* 101
CHAPTER 17: *California on Repeat... Oceanside and Weapon's Charge* 111

CHAPTER 18: *To the Slabs and Back Again* 115

CHAPTER 19: *Just a Kid Named Richard* 123

CHAPTER 20: *Alice in Wonderland, Gravel, and Ninja Cat.* 126

CHAPTER 21: *Spider Monkey and His Dog Cali...but Ultimately Bones!* 128

CHAPTER 22: *Dawgs versus Fillmore Kids* 133

CHAPTER 23: *Flashback: Oceanside to San Francisco.* 138

CHAPTER 24: *Arizona* 141

CHAPTER 25: *Thanksgiving Rainbow Taos... New Mexico* 143

CHAPTER 26: *Peaches, Huckleberry, and the Demon Girl* 147

CHAPTER 27: *Brad and Tink* 155

CHAPTER 28: *Occifer Viktorea Karmama* 160

CHAPTER 29: *So Many Travels, but No More Details* 162

    CHAPTER 30: *San Francisco*
    CHAPTER 31: *Taft*
    CHAPTER 32: *Barstow Snow*
    CHAPTER 33: *Las Vegas...Not so Safe House*
    CHAPTER 34: *Quartzite and Cave Living*
    CHAPTER 35: *Slabs...Again and Again*
    CHAPTER 36: *Alix Anne Beggar Dog*
    CHAPTER 37: *North to the Redwoods*
    CHAPTER 38: *Los Angeles*

CHAPTER 39: *Slabs and Brian David* 167

Street Kids: The Unloved, the Loved, the Lost, and the Lonely

CHAPTER 40: *Kegan...April 23, 2009* 172

CHAPTER 41: *Conversation About the Road* 176

CHAPTER 42: *On the Road Again* 180

CHAPTER 43: *Do You Believe in God?* 184

CHAPTER 44: *Michelle Rachel Thorndike Revisited* .. 188

CHAPTER 45: *Tell Me More, Sam* 192

CHAPTER 46: *Reaching out to Horsshit* 195

CHAPTER 47: *Horsshit's Childhood* 209

CHAPTER 48: *Meeting and Spending Time with Max* .. 214

CHAPTER 49: *My Thoughts on Max* 229

CHAPTER 50: *Summing It All Up* 244

CHAPTER 51: *Coming to an End* 247

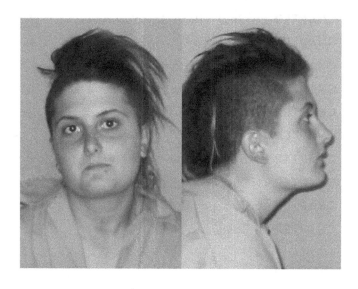

June 12, 2008
Arrest Mugshot
Amarillo, Texas

DEDICATION:

This book is dedicated to you, Michelle, for the life you never got to lead, for the story you begged me to tell. I am forever grateful and humbled by you. Michelle was born on March 3, 1990, and passed away on Sunday, June 15, 2008. Michelle was a resident of Warren, Maine. This book is dedicated to Sylvius, your nephew. May your brother Sam raise him in a way to have the kind of childhood you dreamt of and that honors the kind of life you were denied. This book is dedicated to JaiJai because if not for you, this book would never have been written. This book is dedicated to Horsshit. Thank you for sharing your heartache. I, also, dedicate this writing to Matt, wherever you are, find yourself and choose to live your life, not only for Michelle, but for yourself. Finally, this book is dedicated to the Street Kids of yesterday, today, and tomorrow. May you find peace in your hearts, help on the streets, and promise for your future.

DISCLAIMER:

The name of Michelle Rachelle Thorndike is real. Some names have been changed throughout the writing of this book to provide anonymity and/or safety. This book is written based on a timeline of true events and is kept accurate whenever possible. Some pieces may have minor additions fictionalized to fill in gaps that were unable to be documented otherwise.

I have chosen to include a few pictures I discovered during my research with the understanding that they will be pixilated due to the photo quality of the time period.

PREFACE:

When the writing of this book started in 2018, it marked the death of a girl I had never met and a part of a story that is not mine to tell. However, there I sat, pencil in hand to begin the journey that I had thought about for so long: the dream of sharing memories and giving back to society stories of a life taken too early, stories of street kids, those often alone but loved.

"Street kids" may be a term unfamiliar to you as you begin this journey with me or it may be that you have heard the term but never stopped to give it much thought because you live in your own community where you work, raise your children, and live in your own little world. Sixteen years ago, this would not have been a topic of thought or discussion for me and if brought up my first thoughts might have been, "really, in America?"

If you look up the definition of a street kid, you will find varying ideas and definitions. The one I found to like the best was the definition introduced by Inter-NGO Programme (cited in UNCHS, 2000, p. 73) "Any girl or boy...for whom the street (in the widest sense of the word, including unoccupied dwellings, wasteland, etc.) has become his or her habitual abode and/or source of livelihood; and who is inadequately protected, supervised, or directed by responsible adults."

As I began to compose my thoughts, my notes, and where I wanted this journey to take me, to take you, the revelation that other than one girl known as JaiJai, also known as Wingnut, I never knew these people that I was about to write about. This idea sat heavy on my heart, the idea that Wingnut's life briefly intertwined with theirs and an impact was made in her life, so much so that she shared many details at various times about her journeys on the road and the people she met. It is these stories that I want to pass along. It is my hope to open this world of street kids to you, the reader. It is my desire to bring light and recognition to these street kids who have been all but forgotten by society.

CHAPTER ONE

Introduction

Michelle Rachel Thorndike (A.K.A. Max), born March 3, 1990, passed away June 15, 2008. Who was she? Where did she come from? Why did she leave this earth so young and what imprint did she leave behind? The first time I looked up her name I expected to find more details, who her parents were, grandparents, and siblings. A girl named Wingnut, who I will introduce later to you, shared with me a brief synopsis of Max and that she discovered her name was Michelle Thorndike. Wingnut said she would Google search her name from time to time in hopes of finding more clues, desiring to learn more information about a girl she never met, but whose life had a major impact on her own life. She felt someone should know. This is where I came in because she chose to share what she knew about Max. My desire to write this story is both personal and professional. This combination should prove to be fantastic in the writing process.

Raising children is not for the faint of heart, nor is it for the wimpy or those who do not care. Sometimes I wonder if it is for those who care too much as well. I am a mother of four; so, I have some experience in this area. Life has thrown some curveballs throughout my life as a child to my mother and my father; a sibling to three brothers, a grandchild to my grandparents, as a mother myself, and now a grandmother. I have always bounced back from all the hills and valleys in this journey called life, but my siblings did not. Each time though, I feel different, I feel weaker, I feel lost. Most call me strong, but those that do, do not know the turmoil inside. They do not see the real me, but just the outer shell that is maintained to appear strong. What happens to those who are not able to bounce back or hold on?

What happens to children who cannot bounce back? What about those children whose parents did not want them and so they kicked them out? What about those kids whose parents were too dysfunctional to care for them, but the system failed? What about those children who endured physical and mental abuse until they could not endure it anymore? Then there are those children who "say they endured" when in fact their lives were not as tumultuous as they led others to believe? What about the children that suffer mental health issues that our society poorly recognizes or addresses? There are so many avenues that a child's life can navigate and when parents captain that ship of life who determines those parents' ability? Who addresses their inability? What can a child do? What should society do?

I do not necessarily have answers, nor do I think having government control is the answer by any means, in fact, they fail miserably. Obviously today, in society, I see a government that requires a system, but then that system is failing to meet the needs of children, teens, and young adults who are out there. You may not want to see those street kids, you may want to look the other way, pretend it is not a problem, but the truth is they are there, and they are not going away any time soon.

Michelle, (a.k.a. Max) is my partner in this book, although she has been gone since June 15, 2008. The idea for this book began in 2011 when I first heard the story of her death, but life got in the way. I was working full-time, going to college, raising a family, and eventually enduring a car accident that left my right foot crippled and my daughter with health issues as well. Life is a roller coaster, some people choose to ride a small one, others a larger one, some have no choice at all.

Recently, however, Michelle (who from here on out will often be referred to as her street name "Max" in this book) has begun to linger in my mind. I woke up in the middle of a June night and I swore she was talking to me. Now, I am not one to believe in ghosts, but I do believe that God can impress upon one's heart the importance of following certain directions. Max wants her story told. I went to bed at night and lay restless with only her full name, Michelle Rachel Thorndike, in my mind and in my heart. I woke up and she was there as if we were personal friends and she wanted to remind me of something. Remember, Max and I never met, nor did Wingnut ever meet her either. Her tragic ending impacted Wingnut's life though and demonstrated that you never know when you might make a difference in someone else's life. Max was that difference, but sadly she will never know, or will she?

In 2010, I searched for information on Michelle Thorndike, and I came up empty-handed. I was heartbroken at the lack of information, but decided it was not meant to be. However, her memory continued to visit me, her story lingered, and I could not let it rest. In 2018 on a summer day, ten years after Michelle's death, I found myself sitting in front of a computer one Saturday morning with my coffee in hand thinking, "This is crazy. What am I doing and what do I plan on doing?"

I did not have to wait long because it was as if she answered me. You are going to author a novel about street kids. You are going to tell my story. I started with her name, typing it on the computer. I remembered her full name because I had written it in a journal eight years before. I typed it in, it popped up immediately and I recognized her obituary. Why did it weigh so heavily on my heart, you might wonder? The words weighed heavy on my heart as they rang out slowly in my head.

Michelle was born on March 3, 1990, and passed away on Sunday, June 15, 2008. Michelle was a resident of Warren, Maine.

So little. So cold. So empty. My heart ached and my mind swirled. There must be more. There must be a story behind the story. She deserves some recognition; she deserves to be more than just two lines in a column somewhere. She was a person. She was someone's child, someone's family, someone's someone. I knew I had to dig deeper. And so, I began.

Fourteen years ago, at the time of writing this section, I found nothing but a two-line column. Then on a Saturday morning a little over three years ago, I found a nugget, although it was an incredibly sad and heart wrenching nugget, and it took a while for me to digest it before deciding my next move. I stumbled across Max's mother's obituary, and it immediately saddened me because I thought I had waited too late to meet her, to talk to her about her daughter. However, upon reading it I realized she had passed away five years before Max. The tears ran down my face as I read her obituary and saw the mention of many, many family members. Max had lost her mother at an early age, but she had many family members out there. My tears were sad as I read that Max was only 13 years old when she lost her mother to a courageous battle with cancer. I felt connected to Max suddenly, even more so because I lost my mother when I was only 12 years old to a heart attack. Our mothers were close to the same age, too young. I remember the heartache and the pain just like it was yesterday. I remember the numbness, the feeling lost, and the gamut of emotions that seemed never ending. I can only imagine what Michelle was feeling when she lost her mother at 13, but my life experience told me she was broken and alone. Instantly, our lives were to be intertwined forever more.

So, my discovery left me with more questions than answers. Husband, yes. Other children, yes; there were siblings. In today's modern world, social media allowed me to search for their names and within minutes I had their accounts in front of me, staring me in the face. The husband did not exist on social media, but both brothers were there. What to do? Do I dare to contact her brothers and bring up the loss of their sister who passed away thirteen years ago? Should I leave it alone and let their healing continue? What if they were angry with me for feeling the need to write about their sister, someone I never knew? Would I sound like a lunatic messaging that their sister whom I had never met continued to lay heavy in my heart, impressing the need to be heard? So many questions...and what to do next?

A lot of thought...and then a leap of faith because I felt a push from above. I am not lying when I say there is someone up there, telling me that this must be done.

Samuel George Thorndike appeared to be her eldest brother and so I reached out. I sent this message:

Hello. I'm not sure where to start with this, so bear with me as I try to explain WHY I am writing to you. My name is Samantha and I am a 52 year old mother of four. Many years ago, I heard a story about a girl named Michelle Rachelle Thorndike and her sad death in 2008. This story was told to me by a friend of a friend. I said at that time that I needed to write a book about street kids and specifically focus on Michelle. Why? I don't know. It was a feeling. I started that book. I think that was in 2011... however, life got in the way with family, education, work, and eventually a car accident. Life has really been put on hold for awhile. Anyway, the last few weeks, I have fallen asleep and Michelle...a.k.a. Max as called on the streets has been weighing heavy on my mind. I've been waking up with her in my first thoughts of the day. I don't know why and really cannot explain it. I am hoping you are her brother and I am not just rambling to a stranger. In trying to research, I understand that Michelle's mother (and possibly yours if I'm right on who you are) passed away before Michelle. I am so sorry to hear this. Please, if you are Michelle's brother, I would love to learn more about her and her life and anything you can and are willing to share. In return, I will tell you the story I know, which isn't much, only if you want to know. Thank you in advance for your patience reading this and please, let me know if you are indeed the Samuel Thorndike I am looking for. Thank you.

If you are, I want to also say how sorry I am for your losses. My family has had a tremendous share of loss as well, starting with my brother when I was nine and my mother when I was 12 years old, so I do understand. I've lost another brother since, along with other family members. Life is short, Michelle's was shorter and I feel there's a story there that might make an impact on someone's life. Thank you.

I sent that message at 6:57 A.M. and immediately shut my computer down, thinking I was crazy for even sending it. I jumped up, leaving my computer behind and going about my day, but Max continued to weigh heavy on my mind. I stood at an auction watching materialistic items sell but continued to look down at my phone and think about Max and all that she had missed out on. My phone dinged. It was a message from Sam. I read it and felt a sense of joy that was unexplainable. He was indeed her brother, and his response was as follows:

Hey I am Michelle's brother and willing to share any details I can about her with you, please feel free to ask anything. I think it's amazing you are working on a book about her!! Her death was very much forgotten by most to the point where I can't even find an article about it.

I immediately messaged back, telling him I would answer shortly because I was at an auction. I left early and headed home anxious to write to him.

Michelle's brother was so forthcoming and so willing to tell me everything about her and their life. My mind went on overload, and I shut down after everything I heard. Too much information and who do I think I am to think I can write something of such magnitude: something about some girl I never met. I walked away. The truth is life got in the way. You see, I am an educator, and the new school year had begun. I found myself focused on the school year and other aspects of my life, but I can honestly say that Michelle Thorndike was never far from the surface of my mind. It was as if Michelle was demanding to be heard. I continued to tell myself this is ridiculous, why me? I believed that "this too would pass" and I needed to just move on. But I couldn't. I cannot... whatever the story, whatever the "reason," whether I am qualified or not. I have been chosen to research, to write, to reveal this story of, "Street Kids." As I sit here before the computer, I have no idea where this is going, what the next page will reveal to you, but I do know that Michelle keeps giving me permission to tell her story and her family has generously agreed.

CHAPTER 2

Just Like Any Other Kid

Michelle was the oldest of three children and a role model to her two younger brothers. Her middle brother Sam was quick to say that Michelle was his favorite person in the world while growing up. She was described as an uncoordinated, "girly girl" in her younger years, the typical little girl who loved American Dolls, horses, and little model living rooms that you could refurnish and design. As I listened to this description, I envisioned my childhood, my daughters,' and several other girls I have known and I realized that yes, in fact, Michelle was simply the average little girl with a life much like that of many others. I then pondered the word, "choices" as I have done numerous times over my adult years and I always seem to land on, "it's the choices we make." Sure, I think situations often influence our choices, and "other peoples' choices" influence ours as well, but I am a firm believer that it does NOT matter where you come from, what matters is where you go. I believe Michelle was desperately trying to get there, but her choices got in the way, choices influenced by life's happenings, other people, and a little desperation. You see, as I mentioned before, I am quite certain she was broken and alone. She was searching.

July 12, 2003, Sylvia E. Thorndike, mother to three, passed away from colon cancer. Sylvia was recognized as a hard worker, a great mother, and an all-around good person. She worked hard to raise her children and would not have wanted their lives to have been full of tumultuous times. I am not privy to the details and even if I were, I do not think it my place to write about her parents in great detail, so I will limit it to what I feel needs to be known to share Michelle's story. Michelle's mother was like a single mother, raising their children while her husband worked as an offshore scallop boat captain out of New Bedford, Massachusetts. I believe it when I hear that Slyvia Thorndike was a strong woman because I feel a connection as I raised my own children while my husband worked on the road. Sylvia's husband, Wendell would be gone for three weeks at a time and then come back for a few days to spend time with the family, and then off and gone again.

Sylvia became ill in 2001 and when she passed away in 2003 Wendell was faced with taking care of children he hardly knew. Sadly, his cocaine and alcohol addictions were demons he could not put aside, and the Thorndike children found themselves kicked out on the street at ages 17, 14, and 12, so that their dad could continue to live his party, fishing, lifestyle. As I sit before my computer again, dwelling on this event my mind struggles with the idea of putting your child and/or children out on the street at any age, but also, I struggle with the knowledge that there are so many children on the streets either by someone else's "choice" or by their own "choice." Street kids…an untold epidemic in America.

Michelle was 13 when her precious mother passed away. So, what happened between the ages of 13 and 17 in her world and how did it get her to the point of being thrown out onto the streets? Was she physically kicked out or was life so difficult that it got to the point that she could not take it anymore? Where were the adults in her world that should have recognized her hurt, her suffering? Did no one see the situation with her father or was it that no one cared? Why did she fall through the cracks, why did all three of these children fall through the cracks in society today?

She was a child who had lost her identity by losing her role model. She was a child who had no one to turn to, who felt alone, felt lost, and felt hopeless. This is what I think Michelle felt when her mom passed away and the only "choice" she felt she had was to act out, become extreme. Now, I am absolutely no expert in this area, nor do I pretend to be, but I understand and think that if many reflect on their own families, and they think long and hard, they will see (if they are willing to admit it) these same connections for different reasons in their own families (loss of a parent, parent's loss of income, loss of a sibling, divorce, move, etc.…). Oftentimes children are overlooked when these events occur because the adults are so busy adulting and fail to recognize the impact that situations have on the children involved. Sometimes we take the adage, "They are just children" to heart and our society needs to recognize more clearly that children are affected and damaged as much if not more so from the tragic events that life's journey often throws our way.

Michelle lost her mom, her primary caregiver, the person who showed her unconditional love and suddenly found herself with a parent who did not know how to parent, had addiction problems of his own, and was physically and mentally abusive. Michelle rebelled. Heck, I think I am safe in saying that all three children rebelled in their own way, dealing with what life had thrown at them in the only ways they knew how. Michelle began to act out, she fell into the punk scene which was accepting of her as "a broken individual" and she began "cutting" herself to feel "alive." Again, I am not an expert. I write what I feel, and I believe what I am told. I swear sometimes I am not in control of my own keyboard. The words are escaping so quickly, and my fingers are flying…I do not even have time to review what I write before the next words are formed. Michelle wanted her normal life, a normal childhood, but she could not have it. She wanted a home and family, but it was taken from her, and she was left at a disadvantage and at an age that "choices" are not always made wisely. The day her father blew up at her about her appearance was the day Michelle walked out the door. I wish I could have been a small ant in her backpack that day she took to the road. I wish I could have listened to her thoughts, shared in her fears, and been given insight into her decisions, but it is too late. She is gone. It is my hope that this story will impact someone, somewhere, and make a difference. That is what I believe Michelle would want, too.

CHAPTER 3

Horsshit

I dreamt I met him last night. I reached out and instead of calling and conversing on the phone he showed up at my door. I was scared, I was not going to lie. I was horrified at the idea that he tracked me down, knew where I lived and most of all that I did not know what to expect. I stared at him through the beveled glass as he stood looking at the ground, shifting back and forth, fidgety, drug-induced, or nervous. I was unsure, but I stood in silence. How could I open the door to this man who looked so… so trashed, so hardened, so angry looking. I remember wondering how I knew it was him, but I did. He had a tattoo under both eyes, but they were scratched out. He had a tattoo across his forehead and angry green eyes. He wore the typical layered street kid clothes and carried a tattered pack that was sitting on my front porch by his feet. He was dirty. He looked old…suddenly, I realized he was thirteen years older than when I first met him in his story. Now, I had to choose to meet him in real time...or not. I woke up. I was drained, but tried desperately to fall back to sleep so I could find out the outcome. What did I do? What decision did I make?

James, A.K.A. Stonie, but better known as Horsshit was a train hopper or so I had heard through stories. He had been hopping trains for quite some time. I often wonder how a person ends up hopping trains? I cannot even imagine. Somewhere along the way he met Max and they had fallen in love. The stories I heard were those of true love, those of finally finding someone whom he wanted to spend the rest of his life with. In fact, they were headed to Bridge City, Texas to get married when he and Max were separated in Amarillo, TX when they jumped the wrong train and he said they needed to jump off. He jumped, and she cried out, "I can't." Horsshit believed she continued on and so he went in search of another train going the same direction to catch back up with the love of his life. Horsshit ended up picking a train that landed him in South Dakota. He knew he needed to get back to Amarillo and planned to hitchhike that direction. For some reason he allowed "Bible Thumpers" to buy him a greyhound bus ticket to Kansas City.

Ever believe in fate or that God puts people in certain situations for a reason? When this story was told I believed this to be the case because Horsshits only Greyhound bus ride put him in direct contact with a girl who went by the name of Wingnut, their encounter that started her on the journey she made. Had it not been for those bible thumpers paying his way, I would not be sitting here today writing about street kids. I will dive deeper into the life of Stonie in later pages. This is just an introduction to a man who went by many names, who was homeless on the streets, and fell in love with his soulmate only to lose her before they could truly begin. As I write this, Stonie A.K.A. Horsshit still lives on the streets today (2024).

CHAPTER 4

The Police Report

Yesterday, Max's brother Sam contacted me. We have been in touch for seven months, ever since I randomly came across his mother's obituary. Ironically, I looked for that same obituary this morning and again I cannot find it. It was like a porthole, a window into the past, that only existed for a short while. Long enough to keep my journey going. What do I think of this, you might ask? "It's as if I am being guided," would be my answer. What are your thoughts, reader? Anyway, Sam contacted me yesterday and told me he was able to get ahold of the police reports regarding Michelle's death. He said he read them, they were gruesome, but wanted to know if I was interested in them. I did not have to think about it because I knew immediately that I had to get my hands on these. I needed more pieces of the puzzle, more evidence to back the story. He sent me the reports. It took me a day before I gathered the courage to read Michelle's last moments on this earth. It was heartbreaking to hear the specifics, but at the same time, quite reassuring that the stories I had heard all lined up with what the reports said. Michelle's life ended so abruptly, so senselessly. I want so desperately to help her life make a difference, to be remembered, to be known.

Yesterday (June 15, 2021) marked 13 years since Michelle's death. 13 years since a life of turmoil in search of love was taken from this earth.

Special Crimes Officer, McGenski wrote: *At 2:07AM, on the 15th of June 2008, I was dispatched to meet the BNSF employees at 26th & S Lincoln. They had called dispatch and advised that they had had a train vs. pedestrian, and that the victim was deceased.*

The first police report began. The officer then explained that when he arrived on the scene another officer was already there, along with two employees from the railroad. These two employees had discovered the body, contacted the police, and were there to show them the location.

The officer's report continued, *I then went over on top of the bridge of 27th & Lincoln and did discover a WF* (white female) *lying between the tracks. She was later identified as Michelle Rachael Thorndike, WF, 3-3-90.*

The officer explained the situation, identified the two employees and how they were contacted by one of their train conductors who had "noticed" something lying between the main track 2 and main track 3. It was later stated in the report that the conductor *had called the tower describing what he believed to be a trash bundle on the railroad tracks* that he noticed as his train *had completely passed by.* The two employees were given this information and then *went to this location and did discover that there was a female who appeared to be deceased in between the main track 2 and main track 3.* The report continued with the gruesome identification process. MS *Thorndike is a WF, 18 years of age. She was lying in between main tracks 2 and main tracks 3. She has brown hair which was cut into a mohawk, and the tips of them were highlighted somewhat blonde. She was wearing what appeared to be a red and blue plaid vest with a hood. She also had on white cotton pants with a pair of white olive colored pants over them. The olive colored pants were shredded from the impact and rolling, and were barely still on her body. She also had on a black belt with small silver squares on it. This black belt was torn and ripped as well. She also had 1 black boot on her right foot, and was wearing white socks. The 2nd black boot was approx 10 to 15 feet south of her against main track #2. There was also a blue in color backpack found in between the rails of main track 3. This backpack did not appear to have much damage to it and was just lying on the railroad ties. Ms. Thorndike was laying with her legs facing to the west, and the upper torso of her body facing north. Both of her arms were over her head, and there were numerous cuts and bruises on her arms and body from the impact. It also appeared as though her right shin was broken as well.*

McGenski and another officer began to investigate the scene in an attempt to determine what had occurred. He explained that he had located a trail of blood to the south of Ms. Thorndike, a trail of blood to the north of her, particles of what appeared to be skin or possibly bone at the initial point where the blood trail started.

With their initial investigation they surmised: *We believe that Ms. Thorndike was possibly attempting to jump on to the train and either lost her footing or impacted the train causing her to fall. It also appears as though she were rolled causing the blood trail to trail along and go past her as well.*

Officer McGenski stated that once they discovered her name they sent a message to dispatch identifying her. Dispatch stated, *she had been arrested on the 12th of June for panhandling.* They then gave a report reference I.D. number and stated, *In this report Ms. Thorndike did mention to the officers that arrested her that she was traveling through, and was traveling by hitchhiking and by jumping trains.*

After the proper authorities arrived to pronounce her dead and allow the removal of her body from the tracks, the investigators were able to locate a passport in her pants pocket which clearly identified her. This was the step-by-step process that would hopefully allow them to locate an address for her and to search for next of kin. The police reports were all similar.

One read: *During a search of the female, a United States passport # for Michelle Rachael Thorndike, WF 3/3/90, was found in one of her pants pockets. The passport showed a place of birth for Thorndike as Maine. This passport was issued 4/7/05 and expired on 4/6/2010. Ms. Thorndike was found to be 18 years old and this passport would have been issued when she was 15 years old. There was a picture of Ms. Thorndike in her passport, however, due to the passage of 3 years, a different hair style, I could not positively state that the person who was deceased and the picture in the passport were one and the same. I did believe that the person we had at the scene was Michelle Thorndike, due to the two items located with her name on them. I did have an officer run a full criminal history on Ms. Thorndike, as well as having him check our local files. I was told that Ms. Thorndike did not have a criminal history. I was told that Ms. Thorndike had been arrested on 6/12/08 for Panhandling. MS. Thorndike listed the same date of birth, 3/3/90, as was found in her passport. Ms. Thorndike was listed as 5'7", 130 lbs., with brown hair and brown eyes. The physical description was similar to the female we had at our location.*

Ms. Thorndike, when arrested on 6/12/08, stated she had just arrived in Amarillo, Texas by train and she and her fiance were panhandling for money.

Ms. Thorndike was arrested at Canyon and S. Washington, a short distance from where she was found on 6/15/08.

Arrested with Ms. Thorndike was (her fiance), WM, who was found hiding under the overpass. I did later look at the photograph that was taken of Ms. Thorndike when she was arrested and this was the same female who was deceased at the scene. I did check the information gathered from Ms. Thorndike at the time of her arrest and found she was born in Rockport, Maine. MS. Thorndike did not give a next of kin or an address for anyone. I also checked her fiance's picture and arrest report for any local information. I found that he gave a General Delivery address and gave the alias of Jesse Hudson and stated that he was born in Lake Charles, Louisiana. I also obtained a picture of him and a copy of all of his paperwork. I was told that both Ms. Thorndike and Hudson were released from the City of Amarillo jail at 11:15am on Saturday, June 14, 2008. I asked an officer to obtain fingerprints from Ms. Thorndike so we could enter them into AFIS and SPECS for comparison. After looking over the scene, I did not observe anything that made me believe that Ms. Thorndike was the victim of a homicide.

This officer's report went on to state, *I do believe Ms. Thorndike's injuries are consistent with being struck by a train that was the victim of a homicide. I do believe Ms. Thorndike's injuries are consistent with being struck by a train that was traveling northbound. Ms. Thorndike was hit and probably dragged a distance, accounting for the large drops of blood found to the south of her body. Ms. Thorndike's right boot was torn from her foot, probably when her leg was broken, and is probably very close to where the initial contact with the train occurred. The blood found to the north of Ms. Thorndike is most likely cast off blood from Ms. Thorndike when she was released from the train and thrown to the ground. This would account for the finer blood and spatter found on the rail. The piece of railroad tie found near Ms. Thorndike's head was examined and there was no blood or tissue on it.*

He went on to explain that their search on Rockport, Maine located Ms. Thorndike's next of kin, Silvia and Wendell Thorndike. The officer allowed the local officers to make contact first to break the news.

At approximately 7:00am on 6/15/08, I was contacted by Wendell Thorndike, who told me that he was Michelle Thorndike's father. Wendell Thorndike had been notified of his daughter's death and I told him as much details as I could. Wendell Thorndike told me that Michelle had left home in November 2007 before she turned 18 years old. Wendell Thorndike knew his daughter was riding the rails. Wendell Thorndike told me that he had last spoken to Michelle about two weeks ago and was told she was in Wyoming. Wendell Thorndike told me that Michelle told him she was coming home soon and wanted to know if she was on an eastbound train and I told him she was.

This entire report took weeks for me to digest and to process. I read it and walked away; read it repeatedly. I watched as she died over and over again in my mind, nothing I could do, no changes to be made. I cried. She was gone and through this process as I dig deeper and deeper I find increased information about a girl I once knew nothing about except: *Michelle was born on March 3, 1990, and passed away on Sunday, June 15, 2008. Michelle was a resident of Warren, Maine. I* don't know what I thought my researching her would bring about for me, but so far, it's sadness, heartache, and a longing to be able to go back and reach out to her, the ability to help her, a complete stranger, make different choices, but unfortunately there's no rewind in this journey of life. I pray her story makes a difference in the lives of others.

An officer from the follow-up investigation wrote: *On Sunday, I did put out an MCT message to all officers to notify me if they located Jesse Hudson so I could interview him. I asked the BNSF officer in charge to ask the railroad officers to stop and interview Hudson should they come in contact with him to see if he had any information or had witnessed this incident. At approximately 12:15 pm on Sunday, June 15, 2008, I was again contacted at home and told that Shannon Berm had called the police department and thought she might have information about this incident.* The officer discovered that Shannon worked at a local Holiday Inn, and she stated: *they had received a call on a dedicated railroad line placed there by BNSF on Saturday, June 14, 2008 at about 12:00 noon, of a female crying for help. Shannon told me they searched the motel but did not find anyone. Shannon told me they thought nothing of the call until some BNSF employees checked into the motel on Sunday morning and told them about this incident. Shannon told me that BNSF put their employees in the Holiday Inn when they stay over in Amarillo. Shannon told me that she had not actually received the call, that Charro Anderson answered the phone and another employee, identified only as Carlos, also talked to this female. Shannon told me that the female had said, "He's going to kill me, come help me." Shannon said this female did not give her name. Shannon told me that Charro Anderson and Carlos were all on duty then. I did go to the Holiday Inn where I met with Shannon Berm, WF, employed by Holiday Inn. I spoke with Charro Anderson WF, employed as a manager at Holiday Inn, who told me that she answered the phone when this lady called. I asked if there was a specific number that this call came from and they said nothing came upon the caller ID. This line is used as an automated system to tell a specific person when his next train is and when the phone call is received they announce the specific name and the call is transferred to the person's room. They will make three attempts before they stop trying. Charro Andeson said the phone call was received about noon and was from a female who said, "He is going to kill me, come help me". Charro told me the female stated the number 12, but she wasn't sure what she was talking about. There is not a room with just the number 12 for it. Charro said she and Shannon ran through the motel checking and had told the girl to scream so they could hear her and find her. Charro said they found nothing during their search. Charro and Shannon said they gave the phone to Carlos while they checked the motel. Charro thought the phone call originated from the motel but nothing came upon the caller ID indicating a room. I then spoke to Carlos Alvea, HM, employed as transportation at the Holiday Inn. Carlos told me that he had talked to the female for about a minute and a half before she hung up. During that time, Carlos said the female was just crying. Carlos told me this female did not give her name or the person's name of who was going to hurt her. Carlos said this phone call was very clear with no static or background noises. Carlos said he did not hear any other voices on the phone other than the female. Carlos told me that this phone call was either at 11:00 am or noon, he could not remember which.*

The officer from the follow-up investigation then wrote in his report: *I did feel that this female was not related to this incident and did not believe it was Michelle Thorndike. Ms. Thorndike was released from city jail at 11:15am or later and Charro and Shannon said the phone call was received at about noon. The number where these phone calls come from is not known even to the motel staff and comes from out of Kansas. I did contact BNSF's head officer, who told me that this number is only given to persons who need to know and even he does not know the number. BNSF head officer told me that the employees could give this number to the wives or girlfriends so they could call. It is possible someone called the motel with a prank. I have not seen a report of a female who was assaulted in a local motel.*

I feel the need to write here about this situation that was reported and yet words fail me. It is strange how words about Michelle flow freely and this horrific phone call, situation, portion of the report leaves me, "wordless." I cannot imagine how it must feel to receive a phone call of such caliber and to feel so helpless as the person on the other line cries for help. The common sense side of me keeps asking, "why?" "Why did they not ask for more details? Why did they not get her name or location? Why did the people from the Holiday Inn not do more to assure they could give the police more details?" Obviously, I do not know all the details, only what has been written in this report in reference to the possibility of it being connected to the death of Michelle Thorndike, but it leaves me feeling empty, the idea of never knowing who that was or what happened. Is she safe? Is she alive? Is she still in captivity all these years later? They will never know unless there is more to the story in which we are not privy. I will never know; you the reader will never know either. Do you feel the same heartache and emptiness that I feel when I think of this caller crying out in desperation and no one coming forward to help? Maybe, I am too sensitive, but my heart hurts, my mind swirls and even today I pray she got away. I pray that she has moved on and is living a great life somewhere with that trauma and turmoil behind her.

It was determined this situation was not connected to Michelle Thorndike in any way, so you might wonder why I chose to include this? As I read this section of the police report it opened my thought process to the hundreds of thousands of people who go missing every year, the kidnapping, human trafficking, domestic abuse, and so much more. There are scores of people who go missing, never to be found. It took me down a rabbit hole for a bit, I am not going to lie...away from Michelle....and I felt it important to address it. The intricate web of people I am writing about amazes me daily and it should amaze you as well. Suddenly another human being is drawn in ...a report of a stranger, a phone call, a beg for help as she cries, he is going to kill her. Why? Was there any significance to the timing? What is her story? Will she be remembered? Who will tell her story?

The BSNF head officer told the follow-up investigating officer that he would check and see if there was a way to trace phone calls made over this system. The follow-up officer continued in his report: *At this point, I did not believe that Ms. Thorndike made this call or that it is involved in this death investigation. I did ask an officer to submit Jesse Hudson's name to AFIS on Monday, June 16, 2008, to see if this was a true name or an alias that Hudson was using. On Monday, June 16, 2008, I did contact Mr. Thorndike and asked him if he had ever heard his daughter use the name of Jesse Hudson or several other aliases given in the past. Mr. Thorndike told me that he had not heard Michelle use these names. Mr. Thorndike said that Michelle referred to her boyfriend as Stonie.*

Another report read: *Monday, June 16, 2008, I received an e-mail from Mr. Thorndike and he positively identified the picture I had e-mailed him as his daughter,*

Michelle Thorndike. Mr. Thorndike also e-mailed me a My Space web page for his daughter. I will attempt to access this account to see if I can learn any additional information. A copy of this e-mail was placed in the case folder. I also made a copy of medical discharge papers for a Jesse Hudson, which were located by an officer in Ms. Thorndike's backpack. Jesse Hudson was seen at St. Mary's Medical Center in San Francisco, CA on April 22, 2008, and discharged. It is not listed what Hudson was seen for, but it lists his current medication. Hudson was seen by Dr. William Kim and was referred to All Clinic San Francisco General for follow-up and to fill prescriptions. These discharge papers are included within this case file.

Finally, this report stated: On *Tuesday, June 17, 2008, I was told that the preliminary autopsy results on Ms. Thorndike were consistent with being struck by a train. The preliminary cause of death was being listed as blunt force trauma to the head. I was told that during the autopsy, no injuries were discovered that were indicative of any kind of an assault prior to her being struck by the train. At this point, I believe Ms. Thorndike was trying to board a train illegally, was distracted or slipped on the loose gravel and was struck by the engine of the train. This contact most likely caused the massive head injury.*

Ms. Thorndike was pulled along a short distance, breaking her leg along with other injuries and where she finally fell between the two sets of tracks where she was found. At the time of this incident, I do believe there was a train on Main Track 3 because of where her backpack was found. At this point, it is believed that Ms. Thorndike's death was most likely an accident. I will continue to try and locate Jesse Hudson for questioning. At this time, until further information is available this case will be closed. I have nothing further to add at this time.

CHAPTER 5

Meeting Wingnut in Her Early Days

That is, it. Nothing more! Right? So, it seems, but truly it cannot be the end because I have only just begun. Bear with me and the strange order in which this is written. My fingers fly, my thoughts are scrambled, but it is as if the story must be told and in whatever order it comes. Well, for some strange reason, I feel compelled to share the next passage through JaiJai, also known by many at that point in her life as Wingnut. She gained that name from….oh, wait, that is a story for another time.

At the age of 17 JaiJai decided to walk out and at that time her mother thought she would never look back. Although they lived in Missouri, her father was in California and her mother was in Iowa the day JaiJai called her friend to come pick her and her belongings up. JaiJai's mother received a frantic phone call from her son. He said JaiJai was trying to leave, but he was standing behind JaiJai's friend's car so she could not leave and what did his mom want him to do? His mom paused for a moment and then spoke, "move, so you do not get ran over." How is a mother to decide this while sitting in an office over an hour away? Upon her return home, it hit her that her daughter had left home. She had packed up most of her belongings and she was gone. Where had she gone? No one had a clue.

The day she left; her mama felt like a complete failure. Worse yet, she felt like her heart had been ripped out of her chest. Her son described the car and eventually she determined who had come to her home while she was gone and helped her daughter pack her belongings and drive away. She had taken her cell phone with her, which seemed at the time to be a small consultation because her mama paid for it and chose never to turn it off over the coming years of the journey she was about to embark upon. Her mama viewed it as a lifeline, though it was one JaiJai rarely chose to use.

JaiJai's life had been lived in a small, rural town in a family with their own struggles. Life had not always been easy with her or her family for quite some time. Her mom and dad struggled in their marriage, causing family disruption sometimes. She had gone through her own stages of teenage rebellion, too. Her empty, blood-red painted bedroom left a statement in her absence. Her departure left a hole in her family's world and began them down a new pathway in life that none of them were prepared for. JaiJai's mama lives with a lot of guilt to this day because during this difficult journey her focus was removed from her other children too often. She focused on the wayward child and not enough on those who were still living under her roof. No parent should ever have to be the parent of a, "street kid," but it is evident that street kids vary from one extreme to the other. Some appear to be unwanted, unloved, pushed out or left while others choose to walk away from a secure home, from family, from a place where they are loved unconditionally.

JaiJai's initial "moving out" meant she was staying in a community not far away from her family where she chose to continue her education and graduate. That is a positive not to be taken lightly because so many just walk away from it all. For weeks, her parents would hear she was here and there, but never someplace solid. She was seen almost daily, a glimpse of her here and there and then they would hear things, often information they would rather not know. She was living a wild life. Her mama was a teacher in the district where her daughter lived and where she was living the wild life. Her mama knew she had to be cautious of what she brought through those school doors because she knew she must remain professional or risk losing her job. She knew the crowd her daughter mixed with was bad news, but she felt helpless in the matter. She said she would be lying if she did not share the fact that a teacher's child running wild is really a difficult road to navigate when teaching in the same building.

Other students know things and others think they know things and many people would be quick to judge and label you a failure based on the happenings of your kid, rather you had any control over the situation or not. The frustration was daily. Heartache, fear, and an insurmountable amount of prayer were a part of daily life during this time. People would watch. People would stare. People would talk. As JaiJai's parents, they felt like complete failures. JaiJai felt like she was free. She partied in the small town where she was living, night after night with the same people, many who were students who sat in her mother's classes daily.

Her father and mother always feared for her safety. They did not realize the journey was only just beginning. Late one night, they got a phone call. She had been admitted to the E.R. in a town an hour away. She was in a car wreck. They were given no other details. Her mom immediately gathered her belongings, and they headed in that direction. Her dad was extremely worried. He was worried about their daughter's safety and, also, their responsibility in the accident. You see, JaiJai's parents had learned just days before that Missouri had a stupid law that allowed children to move out of their parent's home at 17 years old and the parents could not do anything to stop them. Yet those same parents are responsible for the teenager and their actions until they turn 18 years old. This could be devastating, life altering for the entire family. I sure would like to meet the fool that created that law.

JaiJai was okay. She had bumps, bruises, and cuts, but otherwise she was okay. The moment she saw her mother in the Emergency room will be ingrained in her mom's heart forever. Her heart was filled with relief that her daughter was okay, and her daughter was bitter that her mother was there. She told her mother to go home, that she had no place there and that the hospital should not have called her parents. Of course they called her parents, they were still responsible. Truthfully, they called her parents to see about insurance. Her mother said she remembers turning away, trying to cry silently, to not let her daughter see her crushed spirit, her heartbreak. As she walked out of the emergency room, she said she felt it was a moment in her life where she felt truly alone and at a loss for what to do. She learned later that JaiJai had not been driving, her friend was the driver, and she was only a passenger. That night could have ended so differently. Her mom realized that even if JaiJai did not realize it at that time.

Her parents tried to bring her home through the Department of Family Services (DFS) which truly was a joke. There was nothing they could do, but they would attempt to mediate. They decided to have meetings in her mother's classroom of all places, meeting with them both after school, but nothing DFS said or did ever made a difference. JaiJai wanted to be free. In the end, JaiJai's mother said she realized that those meetings were just a way for DFS to keep their noses in the loop and not in the best interest of the family dynamics.

Word got back to JaiJai's mother one day that she was living with an older man and in fact, several of her mother's local students were living in his house, too. It did not sound like a good situation, but she always had to be careful of her approach to any situation for fear of crossing a line and jeopardizing her career. A teacher told her mama that JaiJai was living with him and that he was a drug dealer. A student told her that he was a great guy! Another student told JaiJai's mama, also known as that student's teacher, that he was diabetic and could not work. She said she remembered hearing so many stories she had no idea which was even close to true. Honestly, she could not tell me how long JaiJai lived with him, but she thought it was several months. She would grasp at any information she could get from students, teachers, community, and nothing would ever soothe the aching of her heart. Was she this old guy's girlfriend? Was he pimping her out? Was he making her sell drugs? Why would he have all these kids living in his home? She heard he was scum of the earth repeatedly, and nothing she ever heard gave her hope.

The story about this living situation was a necessary one to share because it leads to the day that the counselor poked her head into JaiJai's mama's classroom and motioned for her to come to the door. She said she paused in teaching and walked toward her with a sinking feeling in her gut. The counselor told her someone was in her office requesting to talk to her. She had no idea who it could be and thought it was strange the counselor would interrupt her class this way. She requested someone to watch her class and the counselor got someone. She walked swiftly down the hallway, entered the counselor's office to see a fifty some year-old man sitting across from the counselor's desk. She had never seen him before in her life. She smiled, looking at his greasy appearance, jeans, and T-shirt. A parent? She paused, then looked at the counselor for direction. The counselor introduced him. She froze. JaiJai's mama said she honestly thought her blood froze, yet her pulse increased, and she did not know how to proceed, so she just stared. She thought how dare he come into her world. He had already stolen her daughter and now what? What did he want? Did he want to wreck her career? So many thoughts were screaming through her head, and she just stood there as if her feet were planted in concrete.

The man looked directly at her and said, *"I don't know if you know or not, but your daughter had been living with me, but I just recently kicked her out. I felt like you needed to know she is no longer in my home. She refused to follow my rules and do what I asked of her....*"

Her mama just stared. She remembered thinking, "Did you come to me when she moved in to tell me you allowed this? Did you share with me your motive? What the hell is your motive now? Why are you here?" Her mind continued to scream, but her face remained stoic.

He continued, *"I can't have her living there if she doesn't abide by my rules. She has been given several chances and now she's out."* He looked at her like he expected a pat on the back of appreciation or gratitude or something positive.

Instead, she stared at him and said something like, "Good. I am glad she is not living in your home. How dare you come to my place of employment and drag others into this dysfunction." He looked shocked. She went on to tell him she was thankful JaiJai was no longer around him and that he need not come around her again. I am quite certain that in some warped way the man thought he was doing her a favor and at the same time getting back at her daughter. She had not seen her daughter in months except in passing through the halls and she did her best to avoid her mother's hallway.

She heard nothing after that for several weeks. She had no idea where she was living or what she was doing. How was she eating and was she safe? One night, her mom and dad had just snuggled into bed when the phone rang. It was their daughter. She said she was extremely sick and needed them. They did not hesitate. They threw on their clothes and headed out the door to the town where she lived, and she had given them directions to the house where she was staying. When they pulled into this big house, they were both uncertain about going in.

JaiJai's parents went to the door and knocked and then called out. One of her mama's students came to the door. She seemed surprised that JaiJai had even called them. She let them in and then walked out of the room. They followed as far as the living room. There they saw a middle-aged woman sitting on the couch just staring at the television. She said nothing. They stood there, awkwardly, not knowing what to do. The girl helped JaiJai into the room, supporting her to a chair. JaiJai could not walk unaided, and she did not have shoes or a coat. Her mother recalled that her husband hesitated briefly and then reached down and pulled his daughter up into his arms and carried her out. The woman on the couch never moved, never acknowledged anyone's presence. They figured she was stoned.

They drove to a nearby town to the hospital. Epstein Barr was the culprit, and she was dehydrated. They had seen this before. Several IV drips later, they released her and when she got in the car, they began to drive, and her mom asked her to come home and she said no. Her mom then asked her where she was going to go, and she said back to the house where they had picked her up. JaiJai's mama said she is not going to lie and tell you she handled this well. Her emotions were in overdrive. She wanted to scream at her... why did you not have those great people help you in your time of need? Heck, she admitted that she may have even said that to her. She said she cannot remember. She does not think she did, but she remembers thinking it...over and over again. She cried silently, she felt anger rising through her throat, she bit her tongue. They dropped her off at the house. No one came to the door. No one helped her in. She went in and shut the door behind her. JaiJai's dad drove homeward with only the sound of his wife's sobs echoing in the car.

Eventually, JaiJai moved into a government apartment. Her mama remembers JaiJai contacted her wanting her social security card and birth certificate and she took it to her. That was when she learned she had her own apartment. That Christmas JaiJai's mom remembered purchasing her an overabundance of household items, hoping that some way materialistic items would bridge the gap. She did not come for Christmas, but she came a few days after. She brought a boy/man with her. Aiden. She opened presents and he was in awe of it all. Later, her mama learned that this was something he had never experienced, Christmas overload.

Aiden is another individual on this journey that leaves a lot of thoughts for this author to ponder. If you come from a family who does an abundance, who celebrates everything, imagine being in a family that does not. Worse yet, imagine being a child, a teenager, a young adult who was never celebrated? If you do not live it, it is hard to understand it or accept it. Do you agree? All children should be loved, cherished, and celebrated. They make choices that are not always the best choices and yet they should have unconditional love waiting there for them and someone to help pick up the pieces. Anyway, I cannot go down that rabbit hole right now or I will never get this story told.

January, February, March seemed a little calmer. JaiJai and her parents did not have a lot of contact, but they knew she was working to graduate high school, living in her own apartment, and people were watching her. JaiJai's mama was busy with the high school spring drama and that helped, too. JaiJai went to prom wearing the beautiful, expensive prom dress her parents had purchased for her before she moved out. Her mama felt so cheated because she did not get to take her daughter to get her hair done, her nails done, buy her shoes or even take pictures. However, she watched from afar.

It was the last performance night of the spring dinner theater and JaiJai's mama had her entire cast in the library to have a pep talk before the show. One of the students came up to her and said that her daughter needed to talk to her and handed her a phone. Immediately she could hear the stress in her daughter's voice. "Mom, I just want you to know I am alive. I am okay. My apartment has been burnt to the ground, but I am okay." JaiJai's mama said she remembers thanking her for letting her know, she remembers asking her if she needed her, and JaiJai said no. They said their goodbyes and hung up. She stated that it was a long night for her, working, watching the students perform, and keeping everything flowing perfectly on stage for her students when she could not even keep her own child's life on track. She said all those thoughts crossed her mind daily.

She said she tried to fill her mind with other things. A few weeks later, JaiJai's mom had an educational conference in Southern Missouri to go to and had left school later than she planned. She had a several hour drive. Fifteen minutes into her trip her cell phone rang. *"Mom, my dog is sick, and I don't know what to do."* She recalled that she did not even know her daughter owned a dog. Since her daughter's apartment had burnt down and the phone call to let her know she was okay, she had heard nothing from JaiJai. Her mama asked what was wrong with the dog. After a brief conversation and questions, she determined the puppy/dog had never had any shots and had parvovirus. JaiJai's mama told her the puppy needed to be taken to a vet immediately. JaiJai said she had no way to get there and no money to pay for it. Her mama turned her car around and headed back to the community she had just left and ironically back to the house where she had been when JaiJai was sick a few months before.

A vet visit to diagnose parvo, a vet bill, and a drive, kept JaiJai trapped in a car for twenty minutes with her mom and her mom used that time to pitch the idea of going to college. She told JaiJai she would help her get situated on campus, she could not just keep living with people, she needed to move forward. Her excuses were she did not want to live in the dorms, she had a dog… Her mama always gave her credit for graduating high school. Her grades were not truly reflective of her intelligence, but she did enough to get by and to graduate. Her mom and dad went to her graduation, but she was fairly distant. They still knew little about where she was living and what she was doing to make ends meet.

Shortly thereafter, JaiJai's dog passed away and she called her mom again. They talked. She said yes to college and her mom was ecstatic. She said she honestly did not remember the exact time period, but she did remember driving her up to the college and enrolling her. She said they went to local stores and bought everything JaiJai would need and then some because her mama wanted to make this experience great for her. The college was an hour from the small town where she had been staying and graduated high school and an hour from her parents' hometown. They waited to hear from her, to hear about her first days of college. They heard nothing.

Three weeks after her classes began her mama happened to be in the college community for another appointment and decided to stop by her dorm and see how it was going because they had not heard anything from her. She said she will never forget the moment that a girl opened the door to their dorm room. She asked for her daughter and the girl said she had not been there since the first week. JaiJai's mama asked about her belongings, and she said that her daughter had given everything to other students and was gone. She was crushed. This is where JaiJai's mama's story ends and JaiJai's story begins. You see...JaiJai was gone, and no one could get a hold of her or knew anything about her for an exceptionally long time.

Years later, I met up with JaiJai and she agreed to share her story with me. These are the words she told me: *We partied night after night, the same people, same place. I went back there at night instead of going to the dorm (the small town she graduated from) and that is what they were doing. That weekend after the first week of college classes which I hated, I sat and watched the same people getting drunk, being stupid and I realized in the middle of that particular night that I didn't much like or care for any of them and didn't want to spend the summer watching the same people get drunk night after night and being stupid.*

I looked across the table and told Elizabeth, "I am leaving. I am going to see Aiden."

"Yeah, right!" she said. "He's in Montana."

"I know," I said and got up. I headed back to the house where I was staying. I packed my bags and started walking out of that small town. The local police stopped me, she said. I was visibly drunk and a minor. They asked me where I was going in the middle of the night and I said, "Montana."

The officer said, "Well, I'd give you a ride, but you just passed my jurisdiction 50 feet ago…be safe."

She said she continued to walk. It did not take long for her to realize how heavy her bags were and so she started pulling out various items and dumping them. *"I had brand new towels and hated to dump them, so I began shoving them in people's mailboxes. Can you imagine their surprise the next day when they went out to get the mail?"* And so, her journey began. **The journey of a street kid.**

CHAPTER 6

Simple Thoughts of the Author

How many of you reading this consider yourself an adventurous person? How many of you would consider just walking off and leaving everything? No money, no car, no plan? I always thought I was adventurous, but the idea of being able to just walk away really blows my mind. I mean, I guess, maybe, I would like to know where my next meal is coming from. Street kids often do not. Again, I see an extreme difference in the street kids I have met so far on my journey of authoring this book. Some are booted out of their home for reasons out of their control, others choose to walk away for whatever reasons they have defined in their minds.

Heck, I even met a street kid once (because that was what category she threw herself in) that had a debit card that her parents loaded with money on a regular basis to provide for her on the streets...her choice of living. Most street kids do not have that luxury though, let me make that clear. Again, most street kids do not have family support on the streets, they must fend for themselves in whatever manner necessary. I want to dive into some more stories about the journey of JaiJai and some people she met.

No, I have not forgotten about Michelle Rachel Thorndike, believe me when I say she will be forever etched into my mind and heart. I will be returning to her story, but first the web of lives that are intertwined requires me to address JaiJai and her journey until we come around and connect...down the road. Even before that, I need a good night's rest to draw energy and focus on what is to come.

CHAPTER 7

Digression to My Childhood

I woke up this morning after sleeping in... and went downstairs and made my breakfast. Not only did I have choices, but I had coffee, too. Coffee with creamer, fresh eggs, and whatever else I could come up with. My mind whirled about last night's writing... about the differences amongst street kids and amongst humankind in general.

I am 56 years old. I have lived in the same house in the same rural town for over twenty years. I have never wondered where my next meal would come from, nor have I ever gone without something I needed. Am I privileged? I do not think so...at least I do not see it that way. Do not get me wrong, I have not been given life on a silver platter or anything like that. I have worked for it. I have worked hard throughout my life alongside my husband to create the homestead we have today. It is nothing fancy, but it is comfortable. It is my norm. When I got up this morning, I had a headache. Honestly, it is because I am trying to wean my recent increase of caffeine intake to a lesser amount. I went to the cabinet and grabbed some ibuprofen. Okay, let us be honest, I did not go to the cabinet, I grabbed it from a small bucket where I had tossed it the last time I used it. Drives my husband crazy that I am so unorganized, but I knew where it was. I am human…but I cannot imagine waking up without life's necessities. My heart twists at the thought of so many not having what they need, wondering where their next meal will come from or how they will get their necessities. I try to "ease my heartache" with thoughts of "there are programs…there are shelters…. there are churches…" but truthfully, I realize there are so many who go without. Why? Some go to the shelters and get turned away, some do not realize there is help nearby; others may have mental issues and a lack of understanding, while some might even be too prideful to ask for help. I do not know. I do not pretend to know. I am not an expert (I say that a lot in this book, don't I?) I do not pretend to be. I write what comes to mind and this morning I woke up reflecting on the differences between my life and that of the homeless. Again, another rabbit hole I am swirling down a little bit…. because of course this book is about street kids… Michelle…. a.k.a. Max…and many others, but this morning I felt a tug to address this topic.

Dr. S.R.G.Brush

Let me digress to my childhood a little bit. I bet you did not see that coming, did you? Me either. I grew up in a middle-class home, with a workaholic, alcoholic father and a mother who worked hard as well. I was the youngest of four children and the only girl. My brothers were wild. I grew up in this very town in which I live today. It is small, it is rural. I only lived here until I was nine and my parents divorced, but that is a different part of my story. This morning, I am focusing on the early years while my parents were together.

My father traveled a lot for his job, and it was quite common, nothing out of the ordinary for him to bring hitchhikers home from his travels. My headache that the ibuprofen is not conquering is making it difficult for me to give you a year range, but I think 1970-1976 would be approximate. I remember several meals with strangers and sleeping bags on the floor. In today's society that seems a little crazy to say the least, doesn't it? Once my father brought a young man and woman home with him. They were probably in their late teens or early twenties. They had guitars. I remember my mom cooking a big meal because she always cooked enough for our family, the neighbor kids, and anyone else who happened to come along, and man was she a great cook! Anyway, he brought them in and introduced them…I sure wish I could remember their names. Off he went to do his thing and we were left to entertain. They sat around in the kitchen/dining room area and visited with my mom while she prepared the food. I remember sitting and taking it all in… what a life they must have, traveling freely with no responsibilities. To a little kid, I see how it can appear glamorous, can't you? I must say that back in this time, it must have been easier as well, am I right?

Anyway, once our meal was over, we all moved into the living room where said hitchhikers picked up their guitars and began to play for us…all of us. This is where my husband would say I idealize the situation and insert Kumbaya or something like that. Ha ha. No, no… I do not remember what they sang, but I do recall it being such a beautiful, joyous, peaceful evening; a fun gathering and one to remember. I mean, here it is approximately 45 years later, and this is what my keyboard seems to want to type. I do not recall fear of having strangers in our home or anything that made this event seem off.

Something that I always remembered that I thought was even "cooler" than a family gathering and home cooked meal, was that before my father took them back out on the road, whichever direction he was going, he would first take them up to our local clothing store and buy them a new change of clothes. I often wondered why, what he was thinking. My dad is not an easy person to talk to, but I need to ask him before long what made him do what he did. Don't you think?

So, this morning as I sat and drank my second cup of coffee, yes, I said second cup, please do not judge me. I gave in. I felt the need to share with you the extent of my early years and knowledge of "homeless" people, "hitchhikers" and/or the first "street kids" I ever met. So, now, you know that my knowledge and experiences are very limited, viewed as a child in a "movie like" setting.

Five or six years ago, I invited some street kids into my home for a Thanksgiving meal. My husband was on the road for business, and I thought it was perfect timing. Some might say that it was not very smart. I truly do not know what I was thinking at the time. It was Thanksgiving, they were in town, and I offered. They accepted. Do you recall me mentioning in another chapter street kids with loaded debit cards? Well, this is my connection to that. They came, they ate, they enjoyed…I think. It was a little awkward for me as I was a middle-aged woman feeding several strangers in my home, praying they were, "safe." Was I gullible? Oh, probably. Foolish? Might be. Naive? Yes, definitely. Nothing horrible happened, let me get that thought addressed and removed quickly. Once the meal was over, they moved into the living room. There were four of them with one being a child. We had a piano sitting in the living room and one of the females asked if she could play it. I agreed and she began playing. It was not like a teenager who had had a few lessons, but like someone who was so incredibly talented and had performed in concerts and possibly more. It was wonderful to hear that old piano liven up our living room. A few songs later, she moved to her backpack, extracted a ukulele, and began playing it. I learned that her mother paid her cell phone bill and provided her with a debit card. Her boyfriend who was present seemed somewhat shady, but he did nothing inappropriate that night to my knowledge. The mother and child were polite as well. It was an enjoyable evening and when they left, I was glad I had offered them a meal. Days later, I heard that her boyfriend had done some questionable things around town, dumb stuff, and that they were leaving town. I sighed with relief that our evening had gone well. I never saw them again.

This chapter seems so "out of place" to me, but it is what came to me this morning as I sat in front of the computer and began typing. Heck, even before sitting down as I made my breakfast, got my ibuprofen, lingered at the kitchen window looking at the green backyard the words were forming and screaming at me that THIS is what needs to be said next. I even argued with myself a little before coming upstairs, saying (in my mind of course), but this book is not about me! However, as you can see, the words won and spilled as they should within this chapter. For some reason you needed to know my minimal connections, my memories, and my stories. Now, it is time to move on...to move back to the story of JaiJai and where she went that night she simply walked out of town. The night that changed her life forever.

CHAPTER 8

Meeting Up with...Horsshit

She ended up at a truck stop in Iowa. In today's world I look back and say thank God she did not end up in human trafficking. JaiJai would say she was smarter than that. I do not know that "smarter than" has a lot to do with it in this day and age. I think our world has changed and things happen that are more corrupt than back in the days of Kumbaya by the fireplace after a home cooked meal. I do not know though...maybe it has always happened.

At the truck stop JaiJai said she looked around and chose a ride with a truck driver who was heading west because she wanted to go west... to Montana. Was this well thought out? Probably not, she admitted. She just knew she had to get away.

JaiJai made it to Montana and to Aiden. She had been in Montana for a couple of months, living with Aiden and several others in a house. She worked at a noodle restaurant, paid rent, and kept her extra cash in her purse in one of the bedrooms. Life was moving on or so she thought.

One evening a group of them were gathered around a campfire when suddenly they began to have a biblical discussion and a debate about Jesus and salvation. JaiJai knew enough about the bible that she stood her ground on her belief and imparted her thoughts on the group of people she called friends. However, she wished she had her bible to look up more scriptures to support her views. Quickly she messaged her friend back home and asked if she had sent her box of things yet, as they had discussed. Her friends said, tomorrow. JaiJai asked her if she would also add her bible to the box and her friend agreed.

JaiJai kept her nose out of what was going on in the house for the most part, but definitely could not deny it. Illegal activity, inappropriate behaviors, things she did not want to be a part of were daily happenings in the place she called home. She worked. Her box arrived the same afternoon that she went to get some cash from her bag in her room. She opened her purse only to discover she had been robbed. She was angry because she had worked so hard and for what? JaiJai mentioned it to another housemate, but not the one she shared the room with. That night, the one she shared the room with confronted her, angry that JaiJai had accused her of stealing. They had words, but then it ended. The next morning, JaiJai recalls waking up and getting ready for work. She opened the front door to leave for work and found herself just standing there looking out at two feet of fresh snow and it was June! She recalled thinking, "What am I doing here?" She shut the door, turned around, and went in to gather her belongings. Everything she owned fit in her backpack except for her bible. That day she walked out of their rented home in Montana with her backpack on and her bible in hand. Her impulse decision led her to the bus station to catch a Greyhound bus back to the Midwest, back to the town she had left behind. When I asked her why, she could not answer. She said she did not know, but what she did know was that she was fed up with her lifestyle in Montana, working hard, getting ripped off, and so much more. She purchased her bus ticket, settled in, and prepared for the journey.

There were quite a few people aboard the Greyhound, but several empty seats around as well. She watched at each stop as a wide variety of people boarded. As they pulled up to a station in North Dakota she stood up and stretched as people departed. She sat down to wait for the next leg of her journey. She watched as people began boarding, searching for a seat to call their own.

Then she saw him. He was rough looking, dirty, and she watched as he slowly moved down the aisle. Horsshit. People would block their empty seats from him, move so that he could not sit down, and stare at him in disgust. She took it all in. She said her heart went out to him, this stranger... at how society treated him. The seat next to her was occupied, so he moved on by and grabbed a seat behind her. She said it was obvious he had not bathed in a while, nor did he have much. He had a tattoo underneath each eye. Underneath the left eye read Hors and underneath the right eye read Shit. Hence, she learned quickly, his street name was Horsshit, combined as Horsshit. The guy Horsshit sat down next to had been hitting on JaiJai. She laughed as she recalled that HE creeped her out more than this "street kid" that had somehow found himself on a Greyhound bus.

What should have been an eighteen-hour trip ended up being at least 48 hours (about two days) long. According to JaiJai, the bus broke down several times. Had the bus made it from North Dakota to Kansas City, Missouri without delay, the chances of JaiJai striking up a conversation and connecting with the street kid would have lessened quite substantially. As it turned out they had time to kill, and she got to know a lot about Horsshit during that time.

Horsshit shared his story. He and his fiancé Max were train hopping in Amarillo, Texas and they got separated. They were headed to Bridge City, Texas with plans to be married. Once he realized they had jumped the wrong train he called out to Max and told her, "Wrong *train*." He jumped off. He immediately ran to jump the next train and heard Max holler, "I can't," but he was already headed away from her on a fast-speeding train.

He explained, as JaiJai listened, they had a plan if ever they got separated. That plan was to meet back in the town where they were separated. He rode the train and ended up in North Dakota. Horsshit was going to jump another train when some bible thumpers came along and offered to buy him a Greyhound bus ticket. Somehow, the Greyhound ticket ended up heading to Kansas City, MO. before returning to Amarillo.

As JaiJai shared this story with me ten years later, she admitted that parts of it were foggy, but the one part she was certain about was the love Horsshit had for Max was genuine. Horsshit could not wait to get back and find Max, to meet up and head to Bridge City, Texas and get married. She was his everything and his eyes twinkled when he spoke about her.

Finally, the bus was up and running again. Once they were on the road again to Kansas City, JaiJai decided to call her local friends to pick her up there instead of trying to make her way to Columbia, Missouri and risk another breakdown. Her friends agreed to come get her.

"Hey Horsshit," JaiJai called out to the street kid sitting behind her on the once again moving bus. "Wanna get off the bus in Kansas City with me? My friends are picking me up and you can go with my friends and me to my apartment. You can get a shower, food, cleaned up and I will get you back to the bus station when you are ready to find Max."

"Yeah, sure. That would be great." He seemed genuinely pleased with the idea or maybe the fact that this girl had reached out in kindness. Either way, they had their plan.

CHAPTER 9

Almost Coming Home

Horsshit and JaiJai gathered what little they had and made their way off the Greyhound bus, finally. Kansas City...who knew it would take that long. JaiJai departed first and Horsshit was just a few people behind. Carrying her backpack and her bible, she searched through the people and located her so-called friends in the distance who were picking her up. She began to slowly walk, hoping Horsshit would catch up with her.

The older gentleman mentioned in a previous chapter was one of the people meeting her that day. Remember him? He went to her mama's school and told her he had kicked her out? He said he was done with her, remember? Well, yeah, he was there, along with a couple of younger boys.

"Hey Dan," JaiJai began to speak to the older gentlemen. Horsshit walked up behind her. She turned. "I want you to meet…" she started to speak, and Dan stepped up and swung. Horsshit fell to the ground! JaiJai said it happened so fast that she did not see it coming. Neither did Horsshit, apparently.

"What the f&*k!" was the next words out of her mouth as she quickly reached down and helped Horsshit back up. "Yeah, I am not doing this! We are out of here." She said as she helped him to his feet, picked up his bag, handed it to him, grabbed hers and turned to walk away. "I am not doing this. This is what I left behind and I am not walking back into it." She muttered as they walked away.

Horsshit was quiet, taken back, shocked or something. He just walked alongside her.

"Where do you want to go now?" She asked him.

He was quiet for a moment, then he looked up at her. "What?"

"Where are we going now?" she asked.

"We?" He questioned.

"Yeah, we. I am not staying here. Are you ready to go west?" she asked.

"Am I?!" Horsshit responded. JaiJai knew he was anxious to find Max and get married.

"So, how are we doing this?" She asked. This was the beginning (and the end) of her train hopping days. They made their way to the local train tracks, hid out near a station, and waited. The first train they hopped on was an adventure, but one she says she will never repeat.

Chapter 10

Hopping Trains, Traveling Light, and Searching for Max

They jumped a train! They did. JaiJai and Horsshit jumped a train and traveled to Amarillo, Texas that day. I do not mean you go to the station and wait for it to pull in and let people off and then on again. I do not mean you hop on and wait for the conductor to come and check your ticket.

I mean **train hopping,** *"(also called **train surfing**, **train hitching** or, in parts of the United States, **catching out**) is riding on the outside of a train or another rail transport. In a number of countries, the term train hopping is often confused with the term freight hopping, which means riding on the outside of a freight train, while train hopping can be practiced on any type of a train. This type of traveling can be dangerous and even life-threatening, because there* *is a risk of death or serious injury from falling off a moving train, electrocution from power supply (overhead lines, current collectors and resistors), colliding with a railway infrastructure (bridges, tunnels, platforms, traffic lights or other trains) while riding outside off structure gauge on the side or on the roof of a train, or unsuccessful attempts to jump on a moving train or off it"* (https://hitchwiki.org/en/Train_hopping).

Have you ever thought about this idea of "train jumping?" I can quite honestly say that before the day we talked about it, the idea of train hopping had never crossed my mind. Sure, I had seen it in the movies. Fun and daring...adventurous and definitely left up to the stuntmen of the world. Right? No, I think the common society would be surprised at the number of people, hobos, train hoppers there are in the world. In researching, I never could locate statistics, specifically, related to train hopping; however, I did discover the Hitchwiki.org guide to Basic Train Hopping Rules, which surprised me:

Basic safety rules

- Have your brain lucid (no alcohol or drugs) during all time of trip.

- Analyze different parts of train and avoid hanging and grabbing on shaky parts of car (like rusty handles, mirrors, wipers and etc.), which could be broken by weight of a human.

- Take the most comfortable and stable posture during the ride. Always have 3 fulcrums while riding on front, back or sides of train car (stand on two legs while holding with one hand, or hold with two hands while standing on one leg) and maintain weight of your body to different parts of train to avoid falling off it in case of breakage of handle or emergency stop.

- Keep the safe distance from electric catenary, currents collectors, busbars and dynamic brake resistors of a train. Note that height of catenary can vary during the ride; for example, it's much lower under bridges or inside tunnels. There's very high risk of getting electric shock on roof of a car if you are closer than a half of meter to AC power line or electric equipment of a train: for example, in case of 25 kV power line, an electric arc can occur at a distance of 10 to 45 cm, depending on the weather conditions. If you keep the distance more than one meter from electric currents, you get an acceptable level of safety even if you ride during the rain under an 25 kV AC power line, however, roof riding under a power line is not recommended during a thunderstorm due to high level of air ionization

- Watch out for bridges, traffic lights, tunnels, platforms, and other trains if you ride on side or roof of a train and keep the safe distance from them, or immediately get into the loading gauge of train if there are too close. If it's impossible to ride inside a loading gauge of train, check the railway lines for close railway infrastructure before rides. For example, the structure gauge in many subways is too close to loading gauge of train, so attempts to ride on it's roof or side can be deadly in case of collision of rider with a tunnel infrastructure.

- Do not ride on the outside of trains without handles and other structures that allows you to hang on the train and ride in comfortable posture, if you have no special equipment, which allows you to attach yourself to the train. For example, to ride on back side or between carriages of high-speed trains ICE, train hoppers use ring bolts and vacuum lifting pads in couple with safety belts.

- Do not try to jump on or off a moving train, if it moves faster than the speed at which you can run. Before jumping on a moving train, make sure that the car has a handle and a footrest, then run with a train and hang on a handle, and jump onto a footrest, otherwise you risk to fall down. If you want to leave a train during it's motion (for example, to avoid a catching by the police at the station), get to the lowest footrest of car, face forward to direction of movement, then jump to the side off the train and run after a contact with land surface. Don't try to jump if you ride between carriages, because you can fall under the train. Start practice of jumping on or off a moving train at slow speeds (lower than 10 km/h), and then gradually try to jump at higher speeds.

- Riding on the outside of trains is illegal in many countries, so the police, guards and railway workers can try to catch you if you will be detected. Some railway guards, train engineers, conductors and other railroad workers can be train hoppers can be very rude with train hoppers and even can come to blows or with them. If you don't want to be detected, you have to hide at lower parts of a train before a railway crossings bridges and especially large train stations. For example, a person who locates between carriages of passenger train or inside a gondola car of freight train is fess visible, than a person on a roof or side of train car. Also, wearing clothe swith the same color which train has or dark clothes can help you to not be spotted.
https://hitchwiki.org/en/Train_hopping

Can you imagine? Many people make this a way of life, although I feel I should point out that this is usually illegal, illegal in the United States and most other places, too, but it happens. https://hitchwiki.org/en/Train_hopping shares the advantages and disadvantages of train hopping on their site, but I will let you go there if you want to learn more. They also have a mailing list for train hopping, so of course, I signed up and am awaiting a reply. My husband might begin to wonder about me and my plans if he gets that mail before I do. Anyway, back to the story...

Horsshit shared with her that he had been back and forth a few times in the past week, searching for Max, but had not been able to locate her. He and Max had agreed to always meet back at the same location when they got separated. He hoped this time would be more successful. He missed her. Horsshit had already shared his love story with JaiJai, remember? He told her how they had met at a Rainbow Gathering and quickly became a couple. Horsshit shared their adventures, how they had just been released from jail, and were planning to go to Bridge City, Texas to get married, but got separated when trying to jump trains. Horsshit explained they first got on a train going the wrong direction. When he realized it, he called out to Max and jumped off. Max followed. Jumping on the next train quickly, he called out to Max and all he heard was, "I can't..." as the train he had jumped from moved swiftly away.

JaiJai shared that the Kansas City train yards were definitely not inviting of people like her and Horsshit. In fact, they entered through a hole in the fence, hid until the right train was ready to depart and then ran and jumped on as it was slowly moving away from the station.

The whole concept was intimidating as I listened. Other hobos and train hoppers were on the train. JaiJai felt very vulnerable and unsafe, except for the fact that Horsshit was there with her.

CHAPTER 11

Arriving in Amarillo

Arriving in Amarillo, JaiJai and Horsshit jumped off the train and made their way quickly through the fence before the train guards got wind of them. JaiJai's backpack strap caught on the fencing when they climbed through the ripped fence and broke leaving her hauling her pack in her arms. After walking a ways down the sidewalk, they sat down on a street corner where Horsshit…known at one time as Jesse Hudson and known as Stonie took her bag and began to fix it for her.

JaiJai shared with me that as they sat on that street corner the most amazing event happened. In fact, in retrospect, JaiJai shared with me so many amazing things and events that happened on her journey that brought people together and brought her full circle. They were sitting on the street corner, not panhandling at all, just quietly sitting while Horsshit fixed her strap. Suddenly a big white truck pulled up to the stop sign, rolled down their window and dropped a hundred-dollar bill in JaiJai's lap. "God Bless!" they said as they rolled up their window and drove away.

Horsshit and JaiJai grinned at each other and stood up. He handed her the fixed backpack and they headed down the street, excited to have money for food. Horsshit was anxious to make a phone call to friends in hopes of finding Max. Sonic was good for their empty stomachs and then Stonie headed for the payphone and told JaiJai to wait. Before he could get too far, the police pulled up and JaiJai said she stepped back and watched as they came toward Stonie/Horsshit. "Are you Jesse Hudson?" They asked, already knowing the answer, obviously. We need you to come down to the police station. JaiJai said she was not sure what to do, she did not know this kid… really. They met, they traveled together, he told her stories, but did she truly know him? The police did not talk to her. They asked him to go down to the police station and talk. He questioned what was going on, but they insisted they must talk at the station.

Horsshit turned to JaiJai and handed her a piece of paper with a phone number. *"That is a safe house. You can call them, go there, and wait for me. I'll go with these guys and get whatever this is straightened out and be back."* She took the number and watched him ride away in the police car. Obviously, she had no real plans, the trip was impulsive because of the drama in Kansas City. She stood for a bit and then decided to contact the people at the number and head that way. She called and Jordan answered. He gave her directions and she headed to his house.

JaiJai spent the day working with Jordan. He had some kind of cleaning business, and she cleaned offices while waiting to hear from Horsshit. She was not sure what was going on, but she knew she did not want to be involved. She could have moved on, but she chose to wait. They finished cleaning the offices in the early afternoon and headed back to Jordan's house. Several of his friends were hanging out, spending time together, and playing music.

A phone call came from the police. They asked for the girl that was with Jesse to come to the police station. She said she really did not think so unless it was more than a request. They said no, it was not. They then asked her if she was willing to meet them back at the place where they picked up Jesse earlier that morning. She agreed.

As she stood across the road from Sonic, she watched as an officer walked toward her with two Cherry Cokes in his hand. "Come with me," he said, as they crossed back over to the patrol car where the other officer was helping Horsshit out of the car. "Take care of him," he said, handing her the cokes. Horsshit stumbled out of the backseat, looking nothing like the guy that had left her that morning. His face was red, streaked with tears, and he was a mess. She did not know what to think. She had no idea what had happened and was uncertain of what to do. The police got in their car and drove away. There she stood with two cherry cokes in her hand and Horsshit sitting on the curb beside her, bawling.

"She's dead." He cried. "Max is dead." He was sobbing. "Max is gone." JaiJai felt her heart shatter for this man she barely knew. They had a lot of conversations in their travels together and in their search for Max that led her to understand that Horsshit had just lost the love of his life. He was inconsolable. He was a wreck. She was at a loss of what to do to help him, but she stayed by his side. As they wandered the streets, he began a spiral downward, drinking everything he could get his hands on to deaden the pain. Soon, he added pills and crack to the mixture. He desperately wanted to numb the feelings inside. He wanted nothing but to die. JaiJai could have walked away. They had no ties, but she hung on, desperately trying to figure out what she could do to help this drunken, drugged out of his mind, heartbroken individual whom she barely knew.

She admitted the next few days were a blur, but Jai-Jai remembered trying hard to take care of Horsshit. She continued to carry her bible and because she had no other words, she said that she would sit by their campfire, open her bible, and just read. She remembered reading from the book of Job. Horsshit was on a complete path of destruction from the moment he got out of the back of that police car, drinking any and every alcoholic thing he could get his hands on and popping various kinds of pills one right after another and the bible was her only recourse, so she read aloud to him, and read and read.

JaiJai tried to take care of him the best she could, but in her mind, it was obvious that she was not prepared to give him the kind of care he needed. She said she stayed because he had no one else, but she felt inadequate, ill prepared. Horsshit continued day in and day out with his drugs and alcohol and was a numbed zombie stumbling around.

She recalled walking (with him) to Walmart because she needed to purchase some things for them and felt she could not leave him alone. She left him sitting outside of Walmart while she ran in to get their items. JaiJai recalled hurrying through the store, purchasing her items and rushing back out the exit doors with her only focus being to get back to where she had left Horsshit. Exiting the building, she stopped immediately though because there was a crowd standing in the road and between their legs, she could see Horsshit lying in the middle of the road. She ran up to the crowd, uncertain if he had been hit by a car, but quickly she realized he had dropped his pants and passed out. She pushed through the crowd as she heard people gasping in shock and one individual on the phone talking to the police. She nudged those closest away, reached down and picked Horsshit up, pulled his pants up for him, and quickly moved him from the scene and half walked him and half dragged him away as quickly as possible. JaiJai said she had no idea how little ol' her barely 100 lbs., picked that grown man up and moved him, except that she knew she had to, so she did.

Horsshit was still completely out of his mind and JaiJai was scared and knew something needed to change. She needed to get him help; help she knew she could not give. JaiJai grabbed his wallet while he lay semi-unconscious on the ground and began searching through it. She found a phone number. She paused. She did not know much of his past, remember, they had met on a Greyhound bus, and they were road dogs, traveling together in search of Max. She knew the story of Max and their love, but nothing more.

She called the number. A man answered. She introduced herself and explained the call. It was his dad. She explained the situation and his dad agreed to meet them. JaiJai said it was obvious God had a hand in so much of what happened because she hung up the phone and had no clue how she was going to get from point A to point B with this guy in a semi-drug and alcohol induced coma. JaiJai walked to the gas station near Walmart, approached a truck driver, and asked for a ride. She took a deep breath and explained the situation as best she could. The truck driver, Kenny, agreed to take them to the meeting place. He helped her get Horsshit up into the cab of his truck. It was not long into the trip that Kenny shared with her that he was a Christian.

They traveled in Kenny's semi to meet Horsshit's dad in a parking lot in southern Texas. When they arrived, they saw a man sitting off in the distance in his truck. Kenny pulled his semi into a big gravel parking area. JaiJai got out and walked over to this truck. She talked to the man briefly, confirming it was indeed his dad and then went back to get Horsshit. His dad followed. The dad offered for Horsshit to come stay with him until he got his head on straight. Horsshit had woken up a little and asked JaiJai what they were doing. She explained that his dad was there, and they were getting out of the semi and into his dad's truck. Horsshit followed her directions. She got him into his dad's truck with some help from the dad and then Horsshit moved over, making space for JaiJai. He looked up at her and said, "get in."

She paused. "No, I can't go with you…I'm sorry." He cried. "You lied to me, you lied to me. You told me you were going." She had not, but he had assumed. She felt so guilty. The dad seemed nice enough. He came; he appeared to care. He told her it would be okay; he locked the car and drove away. She could not go. She did not know him well or his dad. But, oh how guilty she felt as she watched them drive away. She did not know why. She prayed he would be okay.

As she turned back toward the semi to get her belongings, Kenny, the truck driver, asked her, "where to next?" She had no idea. They had been traveling with him for several days. She asked him if she could just travel a few more days with him until she figured it out. He told her he was headed to Colorado, and she said, "I'm in."

CHAPTER 12

Song of Stonie and Max

A story never told, a loss never shared, a person who never existed and yet I have learned through my journey that her story, in fact, had been told, her loss has been shared and she did exist as does Horsshit to this day. Their story was one of dysfunction, addiction, love, and tragedy. Her story ended but continues, and his story is yet to be written; however, his chapters still hold a lot of heartache.

Jordan was a train tagger. Have you ever thought about what or who a train tagger is? Have you personally ever thought about tagging a train yourself? People, these taggers, go to train stations planning to graffiti train cars with a tag that identifies them in certain circles, a hidden message, and a large dose of creativity. I truly had no idea that Jordan was a train tagger until later in my interviews. One night, JaiJai shared a small box she had discovered she had kept that was full of her keepsakes, mementos, and a drawing…a train tagger drawing with…his phone number! Score! I laughed and said what are the chances that number is still valid today as it had been many years. I asked permission to snap a picture of the tag and the number, and I tucked it away.

One day I decided to message Jordan because I learned he had a connection with Max and Horsshit. I knew it was a long shot with so many years gone by, but he messaged back. We talked. I was amazed that not only did we connect, but he had so much to add to the story of Max and Horsshit. Jordan shared he was the last to see them together and Max alive. He said that he had picked them up on a street corner and they came back to his home for a brief while before leaving to hop on a train. They partied, played music, and chilled. He drove them to the train station.

Stories continued to pour in, interviews happened, and one day I decided to get up the nerve to call that number. I got a voicemail, left a message, and figured that would be the end of that specific journey. Imagine my surprise a week later, out of nowhere, my phone ringing and me recognizing the number calling as the tagger's number. I was in class. I could not answer. I wanted to run out into the hallway, to answer the call, to talk to the person on the other end of the call. I waited. After school that day, I returned his call and Jordan answered. I explained my journey, the craziness of it all, and asked him if I could ask some questions.

Imagine my surprise when I realized that Jordan was the same guy that JaiJai hung out with on the day that Stonie (Horsshit, Jesse, you get the picture) was hauled off to the police station. They worked together in the morning and then JaiJai hung out with him and his friends for the afternoon, listening to their music and waiting.

I shared with him that JaiJai had shared a lot of information for this book. He remembered her somewhat, but definitely remembered Stonie and Max and shared with me that he believed he was the last person to see her alive (besides Stonie). He had taken them both and dropped them off at the train station the morning they were hopping a train out of there. He recalled learning of her death, the sadness of it all, and then suddenly shared with me that I needed to talk with Clark. "Clark, who's Clark?" I asked.

"Clark is my musician friend," Jordan responded. "He knew Stonie and Max, too. He wrote a beautiful song about them and even had it published." WHAT? I asked quietly, but in my head this word seemed to scream. Max…Michelle…the death of a girl I thought was gone and forgotten, but was she? Obviously, there were more who remembered her than just Stonie. I had discovered her brothers, spoken with her father, and shared tears with Stonie and now here I was years later, learning of a song that was written about her…about them. I was excited about my discovery. Horsshit was not.

In fact, Stonie was irate the day I decided to share my findings with him. First, I asked him if he was in a good space. This had nothing to do with his physical surroundings and he knew that. He said yeah, he had been clean now for almost 45 days (about one and a half months). 30 of those days had been spent in jail, so he was keeping it real with 15 extra days clean after that. So, I told him I was sending him something to listen to and then we would talk. I sent it. He listened. He heard:

Days and Nights - Stoney and Max
Written and recorded by Clark Griffin
(permission given by Clark. Griffin to print)

I want to, want to, see your face.
I need to, need to, know just why?
You, slipped off, slipped off that night.
I need to, need to know just why?

I was meant for you
There's nothing I wouldn't do for you
Stop the time and let the clock unwind
And I'll be home waiting on you
And I'll be home waiting on you.
Days and nights pass by

Street Kids: The Unloved, the Loved, the Lost, and the Lonely

Tears capsize your eyes
Close them eyes and let the time fly by
And I'll be home waiting on you
And I'll be home waiting on you

Any time you go,
Anytime anytime you go
I'll be there waiting for you
I'll be there thinking of you
I want to, want to, see your face.
I need to, need to, know just why?
She, slipped off, slipped off that night.
I, need to, need to, know just why?

Let the train come quick
I'm starting to get kinda sick
Sick and tired of not seeing your smile
And I"ll be home waiting on you
And I"ll be home waiting on you

I was there at sunset
This I won't regret
This moment in time
You standing by my side
And I will never forget
You I won't forget
Stonie and Max were riding the train

From town to town
They covered a lot of terrain
Sipping on a sidewalk slam
And then one night
She slipped off a train and died
Now Stonie's all alone.

He went searching for his love
From town to town
He looked below and above
Sipping on a sidewalk slam
And then one morning
The cops told him the news
Now Stonie's drunk singing the blues
Now Stonie's drunk singing the blues

I want to, want to, see your face.
I need to, need to, know just why?
You, slipped off, slipped off that night.
I, need to, need to, know just why?

Stonie got angry. He said he did not know this guy. This guy was just trying to cash in on his story, his life. He was furious. In fact, he was so angry, I chose to minimize the conversation and not address it again.

My reaction was quite the opposite. Pieces of a puzzle I didn't know existed are slowly coming together, providing for the reader the story of a broken girl who had fallen in love, providing for me, the author, a comfort in knowing that there is a trail of loved ones, broken as they are, left behind to mourn her death in their own way. Stonie saw Clark's song as an invasion of his space, the space he had shared with Max and Max alone, a violation of their story, of their love. I saw it as a memorial to their love, highlighting that love can happen anywhere and can last a lifetime even when one is lost. Stonie's heart is broken. Stonie's life is on the streets, lost, and alone. He turns to drugs to comfort him, to help him cope, to make him forget. However, Stonie himself will tell you, Max will NEVER be forgotten. Max will always have a place in Stonie's heart even though that place is now just an empty hole full of heartache and pain.

CHAPTER 13

Manitou Springs, Colorado

As the author, I am supposed to say something profound here before moving on, but I have struggled with what to say. The truth is that the situation is profound and has played out in a way that most people would not recognize from the outside looking in. Michelle's life was impacted by the loss of her mother early on. Horsshit's life was impacted by the meeting and falling in love with Lizard Gurl...a.k.a. Michelle...a.k.a. Max. JaiJai's life was impacted by Michelle without ever meeting her, through Horsshit and a chance meeting, and by all the events in between.

When reaching out to a couple different publishers, one of the first questions is, "Will you share with me what your book is about?" Immediately I say sure because I am excited to share this journey, Horseshit's journey, Michelle's shortened journey, JaiJai's journey and so much more, but I start with saying, "It's about Street Kids." Then there's silence. Do you know what Street Kids are, I ask? The answer is always no. You see, so many in our society do not have a clue, me included, before stepping out on this journey. God continues to tug at my heart to share these stories, to reach out to people, to help them understand. Some street kids are unloved, so many are loved, too many are lost, but some are found. Whew. Does that even make sense? If not, I hope it does by the end of my writing.

Kenny was headed to Colorado and JaiJai went along for the ride. She had not really thought about the "after leaving Horsshit with his father" events because she was so wrapped up in trying to get him the help, she knew she could not give him.

As they journeyed along, Kenny mentioned Manitou Springs, Colorado and how he really thought she would like it there. This community was a religious community and Kenny knew she carried her bible. She and Kenny had also discussed her love for tea which just happened to be an important thing in that area, too. So, Manitou Springs it was, a community that was open 24 hours a day, six days a week. Of course, she arrived an hour after the town had shut down for 24 hours, leaving her questioning her decision to go there. JaiJai wandered through the town trying to decide what to do. Then she met Tom. Tom had an apartment for rent and needed some help around the complex. They came to an agreement. Another Tom lived next door and offered her a job with a Meat Company. They would travel house to house with a truckload full of meat, she would hook people into looking at the meat products they offered, and Tom would convince them to buy. JaiJai said she did not last long with this gig though because her first paycheck identified her as a "hooker," and she did not like that title.

It was not hard to find a job though because this hippy, tourist town was booming and from candy shoppe to record shop she was able to find work, not to mention the "handyman" work she did for Tom at the efficiency apartments where she lived. JaiJai made some friends and learned about Happy Gatherings and Rainbow Drum Circles in the park during her time at Manitou Springs.

JaiJai met Gonzo and Nikki who asked her to travel with them, but she declined thinking she would stay in Manitou Springs for a while. She met Mary who ran a local herb shop. Mary's shop was so unique and inviting. She kept sidewalk chalk out front and hula hoops. Mary herself was always out-front hula hooping and invited the public to join in. JaiJai shared that this is where she discovered her love for hula hooping and her talent. She showed me her talent when we talked, and I must say I was quite impressed. Hula hooping is a true sport.

Her apartment used to be an efficiency hotel, so it was a tiny apartment to say the least. Her creepy neighbor guy had a phone operating system in his apartment that was connected to all the phones in the complex and JaiJai was quite certain he listened in on all their calls. She recalls July 4th being one of the most fantastic fireworks displays she ever saw. Manitou Springs has switchbacks into the mountains, and it goes up to Garden of the Gods, a tourist area. The road above the town, on the mountain, was packed with people, but where her apartment building was, they had the best view of all. She said they sat on her balcony and watched the fireworks light up the skies above.

Two days after Gonzo and Nikki took off, JaiJai was all caught up with work and had a day off. She was sitting on a bench outside of her apartment when suddenly she decided to leave Manitou Springs, Colorado, and head for somewhere in California. There was no real rhyme or reason to her decision except that she suddenly wanted to go somewhere, she was a wanderer, had been a street kid, and on a whim decided to go in the direction Gonzo and Nikki had traveled.

CHAPTER 14

Cali..forn...i...a

Of course, I wanted to know about JaiJai's travels to California when she mentioned them in reference to leaving Manitou Springs, Colorado. She shrugged her shoulders and said simply, "there is nothing significant to tell." I watched her face as she obviously slipped back into time, remembering moments.

"The trip to Cali was uneventful for the most part," she said. There were wildfires up north and as soon as she arrived north, she was being ushered south. Several local firefighters would stop and give her rides, hoping to get her further away from the fires. Somewhere in Shasta County, a young boy (maybe 20), we will call Brad, stopped to give her a ride and asked her to go to his sister's wedding and reception with him because he did not have a date. JaiJai said she went to a hotel or somewhere to clean up, but she could not really remember where. He went to the wedding alone. Afterward, he picked her up and they went to the reception together. They spent the evening eating, dancing, and talking and at the end of the night, she camped out and spent the night in a field behind the reception. The next morning, she folded up camp and journeyed on.

Hey honey…I'll give you a ride…" the greasy looking guy in a wife beater's shirt pulled up alongside JaiJai as she walked a lonely stretch of highway. Immediately she felt a sense of "Don't….DO NOT…." and she said she always listened to her instincts.

"Uh, sorry…I'm on the wrong side of the road," JaiJai spoke quickly before darting off for the other side. Stories like this make this author's heart skip a beat because it reminds me all too much of so many children and young adults who vanish.

It was not long before another guy pulled up with his dog and offered her a ride. What made him different, JaiJai did not really say anything other than instinct. His black Australian Shepherd named Marley was riding shotgun. She introduced herself, squeezed in next to "Marley" and quickly learned Steve was headed to Ft. Bragg to find his friends. Steve explained they had arrived earlier in the week, but he was a bartender at the Blue Moon Bar and had to work, so he had stayed behind. Now, off work, he planned to go to Ft. Bragg, find his friends and hang out.

They spent hours traveling together and JaiJai recalls that it was quite comfortable between them. Once they arrived in the Ft. Bragg area, Steve and JaiJai drove around several lakes and popular swimming holes, but never found his friends and they quickly learned that cell service was non-existent. So, Steve could not connect with his friends as planned and he decided to rent a campsite for the night. He offered for JaiJai to stay at the same campsite. She said she had nowhere else to be, so she agreed, but while at the campground, she began processing the reality of it all. She had no money, and this was a nicer campground than she could ever afford. She felt very disconnected. She knew this was not reality for her. The people seemed very prim and proper. She remembered a group of ladies sitting around the lake painting and realized she did not fit.

At this point in this girl's life, her philosophy was to flip a quarter to determine which direction to go next. She had no destination in mind. California was more lax, easier to go wherever, but really, she was free like the wind in her daily living and that is what she liked…

CHAPTER 15

July in the Slabs - One Way Ticket to India

Without meeting Horsshit on her journey back home, she would never have been back on the road again. Without Michelle's death, she would have never been in the position to get Horsshit back to his dad and would have never met Kenny, the truck driver. Without Kenny, she would never have known about Manitou Springs. So, California might not have been really significant in her eyes, just a journey in search of Gonzo and Nikki or someone else, but one story leads to another and without meeting Steve near Ft. Bragg, California the next leg of her journey would never have happened.

Ironically, JaiJai cannot remember the first time she met Dane, but she does know it was after her departure from traveling with Steve. Dane was a volunteer firefighter from Moab, Utah. He was on vacation and excited to see the west coast for the first time. He was also extremely interested in going to…oh, wait…I am getting ahead of myself.

Dane had been reading the infamous book, "Into the Wild" and wanted to go to the sites in the book. JaiJai had watched the movie as a young girl, but she did not recollect much of it. He offered her the book to read while they traveled. She remarked that his interest in it sparked her interest in it. She recalled that when she and Horsshit hopped the train in Kansas City, there was a Mexican guy on the train wearing a CLEAN white shirt and khaki pants who also had this book in his possession and said he was following the story. She shared that they ran into this guy multiple times and every time his clothes were spotless, and this was not the norm of a street kid or hobo.

Dane and JaiJai, and camping in the desert at this point and time was quite the experience, she shared. There were Mexicans all around them. Illegals, hiding out, hoping to acclimate in.

Their goal was to camp on BLM Land, no, not Black Lives Matter Land, but the Bureau of Land Management land. This land out west allows people to camp up to fourteen days free in dispersed camping. I had never heard of this land before and have since had others share with me that our government rounds up wild horses from this land

and sells them. I do not know how accurate this is, but it saddens me to think of one more piece of wildlife being defiled by humanity.

Anywhoo... back to the story. JaiJai shared about their BLM experience and how they had to drive through someone's backyard to access the BLM land. She shared her feelings of anxiousness and nerves but stated that all the while Dane was very calm, and she shared how interesting it was that they had such different perspectives about the same experience.

Once they found the access point to this desert land by the border, they realized it was sand dunes, but Dane's jeep was well-equipped to manage this kind of travel. As they came around the first corner, JaiJai said it was like a mass of roaches scattering, you saw movement out of every corner of your eyes and then some. Of course, it was not roaches and that is not the best description, but it gives you the visual of what they saw. Illegal immigrants were everywhere, rushing to hide. Of course, JaiJai and Dane were not concerned about them, but the illegals did not know that! One family had jumped into their vehicle and tried to escape quickly, burying their wheels in the sand. As they drove by, the wife and kids ran, but the man remained determined to get his vehicle out. Dane and JaiJai drove by, but after traveling just a short distance, Dane stopped and told her he had to turn around. He could not leave them stranded.

Upon their return, the gentleman in the car was extremely nervous as they approached. Dane pulled out a log chain from the back of his jeep and instantly the mood changed. Illegal immigrants started coming out from all over and they worked together to get the vehicle unstuck. These people were so grateful and offered to cook a meal. JaiJai and Dane said thank you, but they had to keep going. They moved on, but only drove a few miles before they decided to set up camp. All night long they could hear the illegals moving across the dunes.

It was not long before Dane suggested the Slabs. JaiJai said sure. I think it is at this point that I (the author) want to say that I envisioned Dane throughout the telling of this story to be this older gentleman, maybe in his fifties; however, JaiJai shared with me that he was in his mid to late twenties at this time and she was 17 or 18. I asked her if she was ever nervous with him and she said he was a perfect gentleman the entire time they traveled together.

So, Dane decided he wanted to go to the Slabs, and they went. Why the Slabs? Remember that book they read, "The Call of the Wild?" At first, I wrote down the directions as JaiJai spoke to me, and she asked if I was going to share them. I laughed. I thought about it, but decided anyone who wants to go to the Slabs will find them, so I will not spell it out and ruin the adventure. I will, however, share with you that they traveled there, that it was summer, and when they arrived at the Guard Shack there was no one around. They drove and drove, finding only empty desert, empty canal, and trash; finally, they came up on a maroon van and a man named Jerry walking his cat on a leash.

"We're looking for the Slabs," Dane announced.

"You are here. Welcome to them!" Jerry laughed. "Nothing is going on in the summer. Come back in the winter" Jerry suggested as he pulled his cat back toward the van.

You see, the Slabs are a winter place only. The weather there in the summer is remarkably close to Death Valley's temperatures, reaching 120- 130 degrees in the summer. JaiJai and Dane's first experience of the Slabs was HOT! They did not stay long.

It was as Dane and JaiJai were leaving the Slabs that Dane told her of his dream to travel to India. He spoke, she listened and as they talked, he realized he wanted to make it a reality. At first, JaiJai thought he was joking, but the longer he talked, the more she realized he was serious about making it reality sooner rather than later. They traveled to Los Angeles and then Dane went to the airport. JaiJai did not know if he would follow through with it or not, but when they arrived, Dane entered the airport and bought a one-way ticket to India. He and JaiJai then parted company. He flew off for new adventures and she hitchhiked out of L.A., looking for her own new adventures. JaiJai said she has always wondered if he ever made it back from India. So, Dane, I guess if you happen to read this...let me know!

CHAPTER 16

Missouri Bound for a moment... Then Off Again

Something triggered JaiJai to go back to Missouri for a couple of months that fall. I did not ask for details and she did not divulge, just that she went home and stayed with her parents. I can only imagine their relief to see their daughter come home, but I also imagine the stress and struggles of accepting this "new person" who was not the daughter they once knew back into their lives. She was more worldly smart by this time of life with all her experiences. She was set in her ways, had developed different values, and had seen more "reality" on the streets than her parents ever dreamed of.

Let me digress a little here and talk about something I read, just yesterday. On a site for street kids, I read a post that really set my mind in motion. I will keep the site and the names anonymous to protect those who posted.

The question posted was this, *"How do ya'll deal with blood families that are ashamed of you? I am starting to miss my brother and my mom. I've been near them but they won't see me. Maybe I'm just lonely?"*

I imagined jumping on this site and explaining it all like a beautiful ballet and how one person would dance one way, the other would swirl, a quick jump in the air, and a grand finale ending... and blah blah blah...but the more I read, the more it sounded like a boxing match...a punch here, a jab there, backed in your corners, come out fighting...you get the picture, don't you? Let me share what I read:

Person A: *"Hit the Salvation Army, buy something they would like to see ya wear, get a hotel for a few days and "visit" them on their terms....Don't depend on them for anything just be family for an hour or a day or a few days. If you want to be around them, this is how it's done."*

Person B: *"Meh. I find that if they need you to spend money and present as something other than who you are, they aren't your real family.*

Person A*: "Sure but here's the thing about blood relations – you ain't gotta like em but you do have to love them.*

Sometimes that love means wearing a nice sweater and buying mom some Denny's and just having a nice hour. Once every couple years.

Sucks when you can't even do that but totally worth it if ya can."

Person C: *"Terrible terrible terrible advice.….. This is called "selling out on yourself."*

Person A: *"I guess if the hill you want to plant your flag on is "never giving an inch" to your family, it's your right. Maybe your situation warrants it but lots of folks here need to ask themselves, "am I the asshole" because we are all assholes to family to some degree and dialing it down often yields lots of repair."*

Person D: *They aren't assholes for needing someone to spend money and pretend they're different? It's called unconditional love. That's family. If they don't give it, they aren't family.*

I've given and tried, and 100% would rather show up stinky and let those who truly love me hug me and offer a shower and change of clothes if they want to...sucks having to be something different bc of Babylon. Sucks spending your few bucks just to appease the comfort of a person who doesn't love the real you.

FUCK that.

Give them time to figure out if they want YOU in their lives or not. The whole real you.

Like, if I'm trans should I pretend not to be bc it makes them uncomfortable?

Should queer fam pretend to be straight?

Where does the line get drawn?

Should mixed families keep loved poc in the hotel bc their blood relatives they're visiting are racist?

Added: No.Just because they're blood did NOT mean you have to love them.

That's a toxic way of thinking.That's how abusers remain in family circles.No.Just no.

The conversation goes on and on. Street kids talking about how they cannot even talk with their parents anymore, advice given to just stop caring anymore, to move on with your own life and duck them.One comment written was: *"Family doesn't have to like you to love you... be you,but be sincere with them." Another response was, "Acceptance is key.And they are inept.Their shortcomings are not your responsibility, tho.As adults, it's theirs."*

I read on...my heart hurt as I read. My head hurts. So many mixed emotions, so many mixed thoughts, a variety of advice. Is there a right answer? Unfortunately, every street kid's situation is different and therein lies the problem. I have met such a variety of street kids on this journey. To recap what I have discovered of those individuals I have met without identifying them: abused both physically and mentally, neglected, wealthy parents who did not have time for them or interest, loved unconditionally, but parents might not like their actions, parents and child just did not connect nor did they make the necessary effort. Do you see the boxing match unfolding? Boxing to survive...boxing to do their best.... some want to figure it out, others have long since given up. The match continues....

JaiJai arrived home with nothing but her pack. She was welcomed into her parents' home, but a definite tenseness lingered. Her parents did not like her choices, did not like her lifestyle and made it clear it was their house, their rules. Small towns can often feel enclosed when you live there with everyone knowing everyone and everything or at least thinking they do, but after being out on the open road, no walls surrounding you, no rules, no daily expectations, those small towns can feel even more confining and overwhelming than before.

She stayed. She visited. She was itching to get out. Her parents, naive or in denial, never saw it coming.

Tiffany was a "housie." In case you are new to this street kid lingo, a housie is someone who has a house that does not typically "live on the streets" full time or even travel full time but has a place to call home. Tiffany's home was in Wisconsin. JaiJai had met Tiffany at some point in her travels and had stayed loosely connected. While itching to get back out on the road and away from the small-town entrapment she was feeling in Missouri, she happened to see a post from Tiffany where she had said she wanted to go to Baha, Mexico to a Rainbow Gathering.

Again, for those of you along for this reading journey who have no idea what a Rainbow Gathering is, let me share with you Wikipeda's definition:

"Rainbow Gatherings are temporary, loosely knit communities of people, who congregate in remote forests around the world for one or more weeks at a time with the stated intention of living a shared ideology of peace, harmony, freedom, and respect." Reading online in various places, I learned that these gatherings started in 1972 and have occurred annually with people coming from all over the country to gather together. These gatherings can consist of anywhere from 2,000 people to 10,000 people.

As I learned about these gatherings, my mind continuously imagined a Woodstock scenario. Now, I am younger than Woodstock, but of course I have heard stories and I perceive Rainbow Gatherings in the same image.

Okay, so Tiffany, from Wisconsin, wanted to go to this Rainbow Gathering in Baha, Mexico and JaiJai wanted to leave again from her parents' home and the small town in which they dwelled. But, JaiJai knew Baha, Mexico was a leap because she did not have a passport. She knew getting in would not be an issue, but getting out might prove difficult.

JaiJai did not tell her parents until the last minute that she was going because she feared it would be a scene and her mother did not disappoint. Tiffany from Wisconsin showed up one morning and as JaiJai grabbed her pack and headed out the door for the car her mom followed and screamed at the stranger in the car for being irresponsible, taking her daughter away, and anything else she could think of to scream. Her mama felt like she was losing her child all over again. Her father stood in silence.

Tiffany was quick to share her story once they got away from small town America and out on the road. She had just broken up with her boyfriend and decided to take this trip because of that break-up. She wanted to get away. They had semi-agreed that JaiJai would pay the gas down and Tiffany would pay the way home.

JaiJai laughed as she reflected and shared her memories of this time, stating that they were NOT good travel buddies because Tiffany quickly proved to be self-centered, spoiled, and very naive. As they were driving across Southern Kansas at 65 MPH, JaiJai recalls Tiffany slamming on the brakes, throwing JaiJai forward. "What the…" she started to question, but Tiffany answered before JaiJai could get the words out.

"It's tumbleweed! I've never seen tumbleweed!" She stopped in the middle of the highway to watch tumbleweed blow by.

It was the first of many moments that made JaiJai realize not only that they were not a good fit as travel buddies, but also that it was not just a few issues, but a lot of issues and that something might just have been off about Tiffany.

The first night of camping took place at Joshua Park. JaiJai paid for their campsite, and they had agreed that Tiffany would pay for the second night. The second night came and went and on the third day JaiJai noticed that the park rangers kept circling around their camp. At first, she did not think a lot about it. It neared check out time and JaiJai began to get nervous as she was packing up, but Tiffany had her things scattered everywhere and was off doing yoga in the trees. JaiJai noticed, yet again, the park rangers passing slowly by. Tiffany wandered back to camp and began to slowly gather her things. JaiJai mentioned that it was almost past check-out time and that the rangers had been cruising by a lot.

Tiffany said, "Oh, well...I did not pay for last night's camping yet, so that's probably why." JaiJai was not happy with Tiffany's failure to pay and her nonchalant manner when she mentioned it. Tiffany stopped and paid as they were leaving the campground.

Two days later, they made it to a small town on the U.S. side of the border and pulled into a little gas station/store. So far, JaiJai had paid for the gas and the majority of the groceries along the way. Today she realizes how foolish she was, but at the time it had not registered. They stopped at this gas station/store combo and JaiJai pumped the gas into Tiffany's car. She then went in to buy their drinking water and supplies before crossing the border. Tiffany had gone in to use the bathroom while JaiJai was getting the gas and when JaiJai entered the store, she saw Tiffany on the pay phone. She got her supplies, loaded them in the car and waited for Tiffany to come out.

Tiffany's first words as she climbed into the car were, "My ex and I got back together. I am not going to the Rainbow Gathering. This vehicle's headed back north, sorry." JaiJai was furious but did not have a choice. She could either get out there now or go back north with this girl and she chose to get out. JaiJai grabbed her pack and climbed out. She was left standing in southern California watching Tiffany drive off with her water and supplies and the gas she paid for. Tiffany never offered to reimburse her or help her out, she just left.

JaiJai stood there debating on where to go next. In today's reflection, JaiJai thinks that was God's way of preventing her from traveling into Mexico without a passport. A Jehovah Witness lady was the first person to see JaiJai standing there. This lady, in her late twenties, came up to JaiJai and told her she would like to help her, but would first have to call her pastor to see if it was acceptable. She explained she could not make this decision for herself because she was an unmarried female. Since she had no father, no husband, no covering of a man then her pastor had to make that decision for her, but she really wanted to help her.

The lady made the call, and her pastor told her no, that giving this person (JaiJai) a ride was against the church and against his standards. JaiJai said the woman hung up, debated, felt strongly that she still wanted to help JaiJai, but did not want to go against her pastor. She debated longer and finally told JaiJai to walk to the state park that was just down the road. This Jehovah Witness woman said she would drive to the park herself and pay for JaiJai to have a campsite for the night and a bag of charcoal.

The park rangers in this specific state park always kept the best site reserved for themselves and partied at night. The first night JaiJai stayed at the campsite that the lady had paid for, but she ended up staying another night at the reserved site the park rangers kept for themselves. She laughed at the irony of it all and that Tiffany called her the next day to check on her and see if she was okay. Two days later JaiJai decided it was time to travel some more.

CHAPTER 17

California on Repeat…Oceanside and a Weapon's Charge

JaiJai's departure from Tiffany's car happened fairly quickly and she realized too late that she had left her knife, along with a lot of other things. This was a security piece for her, a young girl, traveling alone and it bothered her that she lost it. She had been traveling for a few days when she came across another street kid who offered to trade his knife for some marijuana. She wanted this security on the streets and so she agreed. At the time she was wearing leather hiking boots that went to her knee. The new knife did not have a sheath like her previous one, so she decided her best carrying place was tucked down in her boot with the handle sticking out. She continued her travels.

It was not long after that JaiJai found herself at a place called Raven's Project. This center was for homeless youth, twenty-one and younger, who needed a place to take a shower, cook a meal, pick up clean clothes, and they gave out camping gear to the youth, too. She joked about the bright, hunter's orange sleeping bag she acquired from Raven's Project and how it made hiding difficult.

There were about 40 street kids there eating lunch when she arrived. She got there in the afternoon in time to eat, but they closed shortly afterward, and she realized it was too late to take off hitchhiking. Skunk, one of the oldest in the group of street kids, was like a ringleader and he gathered the group after Raven's Project closed and headed toward the beach. JaiJai recalls that her cousin Jes called, and they talked as she blindly followed along in the group. She was trying to hold a conversation on the phone, follow the group, and keep aware of her surroundings, but she slowly fell to the back of the group. It was hot outside. The group lingered at some bleachers in an amphitheater for a while to rest and JaiJai sat down to continue her conversation on the phone. The group moved up onto the stage of the amphitheater where it was cooler and they began passing around joints, smoke bowls, and other drugs.

Suddenly, someone screamed "SIX UP" and JaiJai, who was still sitting on the bleachers talking on the telephone, watched as Skunk grabbed up all the drugs and paraphernalia and threw them in his lap. As the officers approached, JaiJai told her cousin she needed to let her go.

The officer said, "Skunk, what's going on here?"

Skunk said, "Officer, I've been trying to get these people to smoke with me, but I can't get any of them to do it."

The police decided to search everyone, one at a time. They patted all of them down. JaiJai said it was a weird scenario because she was in the back, and she watched as the first kids to be searched walked across the way to a McDonald's Kiosk and light up while waiting for the rest. The police were not too far away, and they were already back to their drugs.

When the female officer got to JaiJai and patted her down, you probably already figured out what they found, right? A knife tucked in her boot and the officer was upset. JaiJai tried to explain it was for her own security, a female on the streets alone and that she did not even know one of these kids, but she had just been following behind.

"It doesn't matter," the officer snapped. "You broke the law."

JaiJai was pissed. She ended up with a concealed weapons charge and a court date because she was following a group of street kids blindly. That same group who was standing over at McDonald's getting high while the police finished their search.

She stayed with some of the people from the group that night on the street and one of the street kids let his dog sleep with JaiJai in her tent since she no longer had her knife, hoping that would help her feel safer. This was JaiJai's first encounter with a road dog.

CHAPTER 18

To the Slabs and Back Again

JaiJai's court case was not for several months, so she decided to go to The Slabs and come back for her court date. Remember, she and Dane had visited the Slabs in the summer, and she was interested in seeing them in the winter. While at The Slabs she did a lot of odd jobs, cleaning RV's and running errands. Right before returning for her court date, she was paid one hundred dollars. She tucked it in her back pocket for safety.

She went into the courtroom and waited and waited and waited. As the judge went through case after case, she wondered when her turn would be. Finally, he was done. She was still sitting. They discovered that the ticket had been filed wrong and had been put into traffic court instead of as a walking violation.

The judge read the officer's report and asked, "Why did you search her?"

The officer replied, "Traveler's wearing baggy clothes usually carry dangerous weapons."

JaiJai quickly learned it was illegal for the officer to search her. Of course, this information came too late, and too late to realize that the police officer did not have a real case against her. Jaiai was standing there before the judge.

The judge looked at JaiJai and asked, "Was that your knife?"

JaiJai pondered a moment, and her honest side came out. "Yes."

The judge told her had she denied it, she could have walked away with no charges; however, as it was, he charged her and fined her for the ownership of an excessive knife with no sheath which was a hundred dollar fine. JaiJai shared that it was a God thing and that a complete peace came over her as she pulled out the hundred-dollar bill, paid her fine and left the building. She headed over to the pier at Oceanside and that is where she met Bones.

Author's Note: I feel I must mention here how it irritates me that our court system punished an individual for telling the truth and then admitted to her that if she had lied, she would have been free without cost. What is wrong with our system? Is that not teaching the opposite of what we want for our society by teaching them to lie is the better option? It makes my heart hurt to hear that a judge told her had she lied she would have gotten off Scot free.

Rabbit hole alert! Rabbit hole alert! We had a neighbor once who rented a house on the block in front of us. We had a small acreage with some farm animals on the edge of town. Our daughter lost several chickens on a few different occasions, and we thought it was just wildlife getting through the fence. One day, my daughter called me at work bawling. Her pet chickens had been killed. Every. Single. One. of. Them. She was devastated and unconsolable. That night at dinner we talked about the bloodbath we came home to, how we were not home enough to catch the culprit, and how something needed to change. We began discussing home security and soon thereafter we had a better security system than the local jail. At first, I was reluctant to have so many cameras, but eventually it became comfortable and truthfully just forgotten. Until a little over a year later when another call came in as I was driving home from work. My daughter, screaming and bawling that every chicken was dead, again. I called my husband during the last few miles of my drive, and he reminded me I could check the cameras. I came in and tried to console my daughter briefly, but then excused myself to the computer room where multiple monitors existed. I pulled up the camera that was focused directly on the chicken pen. I located the date, the approximate time, and then I pressed play. Imagine my surprise and shock when I watched the neighbor man in his red shorts and muck boots climbing over our chicken fence, crushing it down, and ripping one of our chickens out of his dog's mouth as his other dog chased our babies around the pen, chomping at them. As he ripped the chicken out of the dog's mouth and flung it, the dog lunged for another and began mutilating it. This went on and on as I sat, horrified, and honestly confused. Why hadn't they contacted me?

I went back upstairs, consoled my daughter some more in hopes that they would call and admit to their dog's crime. Nothing. Finally, I went back downstairs and located their phone number. No answer. I called a friend of a friend and was given his wife's cell phone number. I called. She answered. I explained that I was calling about our chickens and her dogs. She blew up at me and started screaming at me. "Why are you blaming our dogs? We have not been home. My mom had open heart surgery today...." and on and on. I just listened. Out of respect (for her mom) I shut down. She did not need more stress and I remembered she was very pregnant. I told her to have a conversation with her husband and we would talk later. I did not really know these people, but it was a small town and so we all had connections.

The next day, I called back. She answered. I explained that her dogs had killed our chickens, and I wanted an apology for our daughter because they were more than just chickens, they were her pets. I also wanted to be reimbursed for their cost. She yelled and cussed at me, screamed her dogs did not kill our chickens and how dare I call and accuse them. I could not get a word in edgewise and soon she hung up on me. I called my husband and explained the situation. He told me to wait, and he would talk to her husband on Friday when he came home.

Friday came and we were headed out to eat when my husband saw the neighbor was home. We pulled in their drive, and he went to the house, leaving me to wait in the car. I rolled the window down. She came to the door and my husband asked to speak to her husband. Neither of us knew his name at that point. They both returned to the door and stepped out onto the front porch. I will never forget my husband's next words, "Do you have raisins or coconuts?" He looked the husband directly in the eye and the man just looked down. The wife stepped up and demanded to know what that meant. My husband explained that their dogs had killed our chickens, we had proof, and that all he wanted was an apology to his wife for their behavior, an apology to his daughter for the loss of her pets, and reimbursement. The wife began yelling at him like she yelled at me on the telephone a couple of days before. My husband calmly turned to her husband and asked directly, "Do you have anything to say, or should I go to the station and file a police report?" Her husband dropped his head and said, "Do what you have to do man, do what you have to do."

We did. We contacted the local police, and they came to our home. In fact, that is how I know our security system is better than the local jail. The police oohed and ahhhed over our system as they watched the neighbor, plain as day, climb our fence and break it down. They saw his dog kill our chickens and his attempt to free our chickens as his other dog attacked our baby chicks.

"You have him red handed. What do you want us to do?" The officer looked at my husband first and then at me. Darn my soft heart! All that kept going through my mind was she is very pregnant.... her mom just had heart surgery.... obviously, her husband is a jerk.... The officer asked again, "Do you want to press charges?"

I looked at my husband and said, "Honestly, I just want an apology to our daughter and reimbursed." My husband shook his head in agreement. The officer responded, "Okay, we will go over and let him know."

Less than an hour later, the husband pulled his vehicle into our driveway. My husband, daughter, and I were all three out in the drive doing different things. He climbed out of his vehicle and headed our direction saying, "Man, why didn't you tell me you had me on camera…why didn't you tell me it was black and white, I deal with black and white, not gray. If I had known that I'd have admitted to it." He reached out and handed me a check. I took it, he turned around and left. I was stunned by such a comment and did not even realize he had not apologized to our daughter until he was long gone. I remember I just shook my head in frustration, tucked the forty-dollar check on the visor of my car and went back to work in the yard.

Several hours later, the officer came back to our house and pulled in the drive. He told my husband he just wanted to check and see if things were taken care of. My husband said he guessed so, the man had not apologized to our daughter, but my husband said he was done with it. The officer then said to my husband, "Well, he was darn lucky you all didn't press charges," he laughed and continued, "because if you had he would have lost his job." I turned from where I was working in the yard and asked, "What is his job?" The officer said, "He's a parole officer for the state of Missouri." Really? Really.

What does this say about this human being? His words of "why didn't you tell me it was black and white; I deal with black and white and not gray" haunted me for a long time to come. This man worked with the parolees of Missouri teaching them…what? WHAT? The same thing that the judge expressed to JaiJai. And today this same man works with juveniles. What is he teaching them? Okay, sorry about that rabbit hole, but those are two examples of craziness in our system, two people who are in positions to teach wisely, but chose poorly. My heart hurts. Oh, and by the way…the forty-dollar check…was written on a closed account. No surprise!

Let us get back to JaiJai. She left the courthouse that day and headed to the Oceanside pier where she met Bones.

CHAPTER 19

Just a Kid Named Richard

Oceanside had a Boardwalk full of amusement rides. It was a great place to spange for money. Another "street kid slang" that you might not be familiar with, but I am quite certain you have heard of panhandling, right? It is pretty much the same. There is also "flying a sign" which means holding up a sign. Street kids would make money by flying a sign, busking (playing) their music or talents or selling palm leaf flowers or other art creations. JaiJai first saw these palm leaf flower designs when she met an elderly gentleman at the Boardwalk. He was a homebum who had lived under the pier for twenty to thirty years. His name was Bones. Bones was incredibly talented in his art and was more than willing to teach anyone who wanted to learn. JaiJai thought back in silence for a moment, and I sat and watched her quietly.

Finally, she spoke, "Horsshit is the only other person I have ever known that made palm leaf designs."

JaiJai first met Richard at Oceanside, too. She said he was very hyper and very annoying. He was one member of a group of street kids who would go to the Boardwalk to make money or to spange up wristbands for the amusement park when people were done with them so the group of street kids could enter the park for free and could ride the rides.

Richard's story:

Again, a reminder that when she first met Richard, he was very hyper and annoying. She quickly learned that his parents were addicts and could not raise him. Richard went to live with his uncle who was in his sixties and living with three or four other men. When his uncle got to where he could not care for Richard anymore, Richard moved out. Richard was high strung, JaiJai recalls, yet again. Their encounter, though brief, will linger forever in her mind and haunt her thoughts with sorrow.

JaiJai spanged up bands with this group and hung with them at the park. As they stood in a line at the amusement park, Richard bounced off the walls, JaiJai recalled. "There were a lot of us in line and he was bouncing from wall to wall when suddenly he reached out and snatched my necklace. I was pissed and, in an instant, I became very rude and mean to him. I tore him down" she spoke with regret.

"In hindsight I see he was craving attention, that he may have even liked me, but at the time it didn't register. I reacted." JaiJai paused, trying to recall more details. "I don't remember anything else significant from that time, nor do I recall how the amusement park evening ended, but what I do remember is six weeks later."

"Six weeks later, I was walking in the Haight-Ashbury district of San Francisco." As JaiJai's mind recollects, I will share with you, the reader, that the Haight-Ashbury district of San Francisco is "a neighborhood" where cultures collided, and the hippy movement happened in the sixties. It was home to Jimi Hendrix and frequented by many famous musicians.

So, JaiJai was walking in the Haight-Ashbury district of San Francisco and walked by a group of heroin users who were nodding off along the side of a building when suddenly one of them said, "Do you see that angel? Man, she's glowing...she's an angel." JaiJai looked over in the direction of the voice. The person calling her an angel was Richard or at least it was what was left of Richard. You see, six weeks hooked on heroin, and he had drastically changed. He had sores all over him, his face was sunk in, and he was missing teeth.

"He didn't recognize me. I called him by name. He was surprised that I (the angel) knew his name." She began to cry. Heartbroken, this has stuck with me all these years. I was not very Christlike, or grace filled toward Richard. Did my behavior trigger him?"

CHAPTER 20

Alice in Wonderland, Gravel, and Ninja Cat

So many street kids, so many stories, so many lives affected by…society? Lack of parenting? Poor choices? Our society advocates for these programs and services, but do we have unbiased statistics to back them up as worthwhile, making a difference and beneficial to our children in America? HOW do we have so many "fall through the crack" kids in the United States?

Allison Wonderland, legitimately had her name changed to this. She was crazy or, so I have been told. She lived in a rundown two room apartment, but she spent most of her time in the park with the homeless of the city. The individual who shared with me Alice's story admitted that as she sat here today and looked back at the previous events and realized it was most likely that Alice was an addict. One night she let a bunch of girls go to her apartment to take a shower and clean up. I was told there were six or seven girls. She did not have electricity but had running water. While the girls were there, they witnessed her leave out the front door, but when she returned, she came back in through the window. In retrospect, my sharer of information summed Allison "Alice" Wonderland up as an addict who was demonic and very eccentric all together.

Ninja Cat was a young kid, who was in his late teens or early twenties at the most. He traveled with a girl named Gravel. Gravel had a drinking problem, and it was obvious to anyone who met her. Gravel got her name from getting drunk, falling down a mountainside, and having a full mouth of gravel at the bottom, spitting it out, and going right back to partying. From that moment on, she was dubbed Gravel.

CHAPTER 21

Spider Monkey and his dog Cali... but Ultimately Bones!

Just so you know, I could not make these names up. They are real names. Names of street kids who gained their names through numerous ways. What is their true identity? I have no idea. I often wonder if their identity is hidden to hide their hurt, to forget their past, to.... what? Again, I do not know, but how do you go from being Jason Clark to Spider Monkey? I often wonder today where these individuals ended up, too.

I was told about Spider Monkey by JaiJai. She met Spider Monkey when she was traveling with Bones. She and Bones had traveled up the coast with Speedy and Rocky from Oceanside. Again, are you hearing these names? Bones? Speedy? Rocky? Where did their true identities go and why did they leave?

The four travelers camped together once they arrived at their destination, Golden Gate Park. After setting up camp, they all decided to go out. JaiJai knew it was getting close to the full moon. In fact, she recalls it was just a night or two before it would happen. I found it interesting when she spoke and how aware she was of a full moon and the meaning behind it in her world. She said that none of them ended up going back to their original camp that night. JaiJai ended up meeting Spider Monkey. When she first encountered him, he was tripping on acid. She was sober. She watched as his wild antics continued and they ran all over the Golden Gate Park. He ran like crazy, and she followed in awe, from the Japanese Gardens to Buffalo and then the Science Dome. That night as the fog settled into the park it looked like a huge UFO was present. Again, she stressed that she was sober, but caught up in the chaos of the street kids with commotion and partying happening from the Japanese Gardens to Buffalo and the ever-present UFO they all believed they witnessed, in a stupor or not.

As she reminisced about that night, she murmured numerous times, it was a wild night. As Spider Monkey ran wild through the park he bounced from seat to seat, climbed trees, walked on tables, and acted just like a Spider Monkey, hence his street name. He ran with his fellow street kids, tripping on acid and doing whatever illicit drugs were flowing freely. His dog, Cali, ran closely beside him, never leaving his side.

Two nights later, as I said previously, JaiJai knew it was going to be a full moon. She also knew what a full moon at the Golden Gate Park might look like as she had witnessed it before. The days leading up to it were usually unruly and wild and she could only imagine how a full moon would make the chaos spiral even more. She decided she wanted to go stay at a hotel away from the park to avoid any craziness and danger. Since she was traveling mostly with Bones, she reached out to him and asked him to go with her to get a hotel room. Bones refused to go with her even when she reminded him that full moons meant even crazier with the street kids' scene. Bones said he was staying. She told him to stay safe and journeyed off on her own to a motel just a few blocks away.

The next day, after a hot shower and a warm breakfast JaiJai traveled back to the park to assess the destruction. People were lying everywhere, trash strewn from the chaos the night before, street bums looking even more haggard than their norm, and a definite stench of alcohol and remnants of the full moon parties. When she arrived back at their camp, Bones was not there. She began walking through the messiness in search of Bones. He was gone. As she encountered different people she knew, she asked questions. Many had no clue as to the whereabouts of Bones. Finally, someone told her he got jumped by a group of street girls and beat up. They were not sure what had happened to him after that. JaiJai called the local hospitals but could not find him. She did not know his real name, which hindered her search for him. She called and called without any luck and finally determined that without a name she was not going to be able to locate him. She waited a day and then decided it was time to leave the area. JaiJai knew that when or if he ever returned, he would have a beef with whatever group had jumped him and that would mean she would have a beef with them as well and it might cause more ruckus than she needed. After all, she thought to herself, HE is a grown man. Today, she still has regrets that she left without knowing his whereabouts and safety. Bones was what the street kids called a wharf rat- a homebun. He always stayed within the same five-mile radius of his "home" which might be under a bridge, in an alley or just simply on the streets, but the same streets located in that five-mile radius. Rocky, Speedy and JaiJai had convinced him that day that a change of scenery would do him good. They talked him into traveling with them to San Francisco, so therefore she had a feeling of responsibility for him. She never saw Rocky or Speedy again, either. Looking back, she realizes she could not keep him safe; it was the choice he made. JaiJai repeated to me, "San Francisco Park gets crazy during a full moon, partying, crazy, and all…drugs, drinking and more." Sadly, to this day, she does not know what happened to him. She heard rumor he had gotten into a fight with a group of girls who boot stomped, or curb stomped homeless men because they have issues with them. Rumor was he got into an altercation.

She wished she had made him go to a hotel. She wished she did not take off and leave without knowing what happened to him. She knew she was not responsible for all of that. I remind her that she offered for him to go with her, but it was the choice he made to stay behind. I am not sure that make her feel any better with the "not knowing," but it reminds me, and I remind you the reader that what is important in life is that you make good choices. Choices are what makes your future. Choices are left up to you as a human being. Author notes: My philosophy in the classroom over my 25 years of teaching has always been, "It does not matter where you come from, what matters is where you go and the choices you make that get you there. So, make good choices!"

CHAPTER 22

Dawgs versus Fillmore Kids

Haight street kids...I have pondered this chapter too long and I am not sure how to write it. You know me and rabbit holes. I have looked and looked, researched, and really want to go down that rabbit hole. I even considered the idea of attempting to interview a member of the Fillmore gang sentenced on March 22, 2022, for a pair of gang-related shootings. What got 23-year-old Esteban Reyes into the situation he finds himself in? Did he grow up in that area? How did he get involved in the gang? Why did he get involved in the gang? What took this nice looking, young man from a small child to a grown gang member, shooting at other human beings? Why? WHY? I cannot even fathom the lifestyle, the whys, the choices made. My heart breaks for those who were shot, but also for those who find themselves in positions of bad choices.

I cannot go further with my research or my desire to dig deeper at this time. I must finish this book because Michelle is calling out for me to get it done. Yes, Michelle. We have gone a long way away from her story, but I promise, I will return. She is my motivation for writing this story. It is because of her that my fingers fly, but unfortunately life gets in the way from time to time and my writing gets put aside. As I write this though, I have a deadline and a commitment to get this book to the publisher, to share many stories of street kids and journeys, but most of all to tell Michelle's story, JaiJai's journey, and of Horsshit's life. To share in hopes that people are interested, that lessons are learned, and society gets a better understanding of street kids. Now, back to Haight Street.

JaiJai hesitated when I asked about Haight Street and her gang experiences. She pondered the question and finally answered, "I just know that I encountered two gangs in San Francisco and more specifically in the Haight-Ashbury area. There were older people in the gangs, and they ran the streets. Then they had their neighbors outside of the park. I was told to avoid those neighborhoods. However, the older gang members would send the younger gang members, and even their own siblings to the park to be trained. These younger ones could be anywhere between the ages of eight and fourteen. Their job was to hang out in the park, pick-pocket passersby, control the drug flow and do whatever else was asked of them. They had to learn how to behave."

"If I remember right," she lowered her voice, "there were the Dawgs and the Fillmore Gangs. Fighting between the two happened frequently, but it always seemed like the park was more neutral. It is easy to ignore that it's an actual gang activity going on when you are in the park, but it was. The public see it as some young, dumb, kid and do not understand that those kids are being trained, initiated, and are a part of a gang. It is crazy. I remember that they traded dogs for drugs."

A Fillmore girl showed up on the streets one day where JaiJai was hanging out. She had a big dog on a leash and wanted to give it to JaiJai. JaiJai was not looking for a dog. The Fillmore girl was persistent in that she needed a dog. JaiJai said she felt pressured by this young girl, and she finally took it because she did not know what else to do. She did not want to make this girl mad. She knew she was a part of a gang. JaiJai said she kept the dog for two or three days, but really did not want it and was just waiting to figure out what to do with it. One day she wanted to go into the city, but she knew she could not take the dog with her because it was not licensed. She reached out to a couple of street kids she knew and asked them if they would watch the dog that day while she was gone. They agreed.

While she was away, a guy who was a member of the Dawg gang came to their camp and claimed the dog. The street kids did not argue or put up a fight but gave up the dog to the Dawg member. When JaiJai returned to find the dog gone, she went looking for him. She approached the Dawg member with the dog, and he told her that the Fillmore's had done business with the Dawgs and that this dog was supposed to be a part of the payment. That Fillmore girl had no right to rehome her dog with JaiJai.

JaiJai left and went back to the street kids she was running with. That night, several of them left. She stayed in camp and fell asleep. She said the next morning she woke up with a gang member standing over her. Like a stupid, naive country girl she stood up and confronted him. Basically, he came to tell her he did not like the group she was traveling with. He stated that if she would quit traveling with the street kids staying in her camp, he would give her the dog back. She laughed at the memory. She said," One, he woke me up, two he had the audacity to tell me what to do…who the fuck did he think he was telling me who I can and cannot travel with? I went off on him. I said just that, "who the fuck do you think you are, telling me who I can and cannot travel with." JaiJai said she then went on and told him to take his dog and shove it up his ass." She paused. "It's one of those moments I look back on and realize that is a moment where people die, go missing, or worse, and I really should have, except for God must have intervened. He stood there laughing at me and then he turned and walked off." JaiJai said that by the time she got up, got dressed, and walked to McDonalds everyone on the streets around her was talking about how she had gone off on a gang member. They all thought it was very bold and pretty crazy. And my readers, this is how JaiJai earned her street name, "a Wingnut."

For the longest time after this incident, she recalls that any time she would go back to the park, gang members would hold doors open for her at McDonalds and show respect. She said it was not a respect she had earned, but somehow, she got it. No one messed with her. She said she went back and forth to the park for the next year and absolutely no one ever messed with her. Other homeless people would tell her that they were told to keep an eye out and watch over her. When she yelled at that Dawg gang member it changed the whole dynamic. Even the Fillmore gang members respected her. She sat silently for a bit, thinking through her memories, and then finally she said, "Shot, killed, or disappeared is what should have happened to me, but instead God took it and put it into a unique perspective. They all thought this girl was crazy and so I just played into it."

CHAPTER 23

Flashback: Oceanside to San Francisco

Bones was a wharf rat and wanted to see some place else. JaiJai convinced him to take the light rail to San Francisco with Rocky, Speedy, and herself. I know I already shared with you about Bones, but I said very little earlier about Rocky and Speedy. They were from Riverside, California. They were elementary school friends. Sometime in junior high Speedy had been hit upside the head with a brick and it caused him lots of mental issues. His grandma, aunt or elderly person taking care of him could no longer care for him or find a facility. So, Rocky decided to travel with him because they were either going to be homeless in Riverside or be homeless and travel.

They had all met in Oceanside. There was another guy named Alex traveling with them. He did not look like a street kid even though he was sleeping with the homeless kids. He said he was 27 years old. They were all traveling in the same direction together in a group, but not necessarily together if that makes sense.

One morning, on the light rail, Speedy began to have a seizure. Of course, the public did not know his condition, nor did they understand his mental issues and so immediately those surrounding him assumed it was drugs or alcohol. Someone from the public called the police. The police arrived and quickly recognized that Speedy was having a seizure and was almost through with it. There was nothing they could do unless he asked to go to the hospital, which he did not. The police decided that they could ID the street kids that were present though. As they stood around identifying each kid through their ID's, some walked off and others moved to the bench beyond, waiting. JaiJai was standing close by when Alex presented his ID. The police ran it, and it came back that he had warrants up in the state of Washington. His name was not Alex, but it was something else. JaiJai said they also mentioned that he was 34 years old. She felt all along there was something off in regard to this guy, but this all just confirmed it for her. The police let him go because his warrants were not extraditable. No one else in the group seemed to hear the story of Alex except JaiJai. He went back to being Alex as soon as the police walked away. Once they got to San Francisco Alex took off and she never saw him again. She suddenly remembered that

Max, the kid, was with them, too, during all of this. He had gone to Oceanside with JaiJai. She said he was quiet; so quiet, it was easy to forget he was around.

The first couple of days in San Francisco were fun. They toured the area, spent time in Golden Gate Park and just enjoyed all the people. However, JaiJai knew the full moon meant chaos and she felt it in her bones (no pun intended) that she should not be there during this time. Obviously, you already read the chapter about Bones and you know the outcome or at least the mystery.

What ever happened to Bones…to Max….to Alex? Who was Alex? Heck, who are they all? What are their stories? Where did Speedy and Rocky go after arriving in San Francisco? What became of them? Remember Richard, the young boy who chose heroin? How did his life end up or end? Who tells their stories? I feel I need to speak for them all and yet, I am not sure I am qualified. Also, for me, and for you the reader, there is no true ending.

CHAPTER 24

Arizona

Remember the story of Dane the volunteer firefighter from Moab, Utah? Remember how they ended up at The Slabs in July? Well, at some point while JaiJai and Dane were traveling across California on their way to The Slabs, they had stopped at a Renaissance Fair where she met a lady who went by the name of Evette Wolfe. They all sat around and talked. JaiJai shared her travels and Evette had told her that if they ever ended up in her area, JaiJai should look her up and she would have places to stay, houses to rent.

Anyway, after a crazy summer of travel, sometime around November, JaiJai started thinking that she would really like to get a job and a place to stay to be off the streets for the winter. She decided to message Evette. Evette said sure, she had a place for her to stay in Arizona. They arranged that JaiJai would do upkeep, some maintenance, painting, and odd jobs on some of Evette's other rental places to stay rent free in a rental of her own. Evette lived in Maricopa County and the house JaiJai rented was nearby. Once she got settled, she decided to walk into town to apply for jobs. When she went into McDonalds to apply, she met a young kid who started a conversation with her. When he asked her where she was from, she told him. He told her he was from a town less than an hour from where she grew up. He gave her his number.

After a day of applications, she decided it was time to walk home, but soon realized she could not remember her new address and all the houses looked the same, "Cookie cutter houses," she said. She finally decided to use the number the guy had given her and call him. He got off work and came and picked her up. She said they drove up and down the blocks, searching for the house where she lived.

They became friends after that for a while. He was Hispanic and had a big, welcoming family and she enjoyed their company a lot. Besides, he had rescued her and helped her locate her home…for the time being anyway.

CHAPTER 25:

Thanksgiving Rainbow Taos... New Mexico

JaiJai was living in Maricopa County Arizona, and she had just started a job at a Fries Grocery Store. She had been living and working there for two weeks. JaiJai was looking forward to having Thanksgiving off even though she had nothing planned. It was just the idea of a break; she was not used to working a schedule.

She explained that Evette and her family had planned a big get together and she had been invited, but she had not wanted to go. She shared that a crowd full of strangers was completely out of her comfort zone. So, JaiJai got on a hippy website and looked up gatherings. Ironically Horsshit had told her about these. Remember him?

She wondered about him often and how his situation had turned out. She had left him quite some time ago, but she could not seem to forget him and the way their connection had ended. So, she had been checking these gathering sites in hopes that she would see his name or his comments and know that he was still around.

That is when she came across a "Gathering in New Mexico for Thanksgiving." This intrigued her and she began reading on the site about this specific event. People were meeting up two weeks ahead of Thanksgiving. Then they had three days of festivities, food, and fun planned out. After that there would be at least one day of clean up.

JaiJai decided this was where she wanted to spend her Thanksgiving. When I asked her why she decided to go there, she said because all the hippy gatherings she had been to previously have been great. I, the author, struggled with this thought process because when I compared Evette's family gathering and the Rainbow Taos gathering, all I saw were two events with a lot of strangers. However, something must have enticed JaiJai because as soon as she was off work for the weekend, she took off to New Mexico for the Thanksgiving Rainbow Taos Event.

Hippies do not give great directions. Those were JaiJai's words. Not mine. She laughed at that statement and then continued, "They say go to this road, look for the pile of rocks, and figure out which direction they are pointing. That is, it," she said. "Then you have to figure it out!"

She thought she was getting close, but at one point after walking up and down a road numerous times, trying to figure out where she was supposed to go, she decided she was ready to give up. She turned around once again and headed back to the intersection where she had been dropped off. Suddenly, out of nowhere, a big brown van of hippies pulled up to the intersection. They asked her where she was going, and she told them she was on the way to the Rainbow Taos. They told her there was no reason for her to walk the rest of the way and to get in. She did. She said that they put their directions together and began driving down the miles stretch of old road, driving really slow…and…nothing. They were about to turn around and head back when someone in the van hollered, "There's the sign." Up in front of them were about three or four rocks about a foot tall or less that were the "sign" that indicated they were supposed to drive randomly through the desert in that direction.

Off they went, a van full of hippies in search of a Thanksgiving Rainbow Taos. Just a few miles one direction and a few more another and they discovered the big gathering out on BLM land (Bureau of Land Management). Someone had pulled in a mobile trailer. They did not own the land, but there were so many people there. At least 500 people were there with their RV's, tents, and hammocks. JaiJai said it was an amazing experience to witness all of these families gathered together in one place to have their Thanksgiving. She smiled and chuckled as she shared more memories. "People were trying to shove big turkeys in small ovens. There was one large tent for the main gathering. The drum circles played for three days straight in that tent. It was amazing. It was an incredibly enjoyable experience with LOTS of free-flowing marijuana. Everything that was cooked had ganja butter in it." Are you googling that recipe? I had to look it up.

She said she remembered sitting in the main area watching the original hippies from the sixties playing cards. She said they all had crazy names and were talking about Woodstock. These people had stories that were amazing. The old men gave the young kids a tough time about having too much energy and being up all night.

This is where JaiJai first met Peaches. (When I first met Peaches on her journey, I assumed Peaches was a girl. This is a lesson to never assume.) It snowed the night before Thanksgiving and a lot of people in individual tents ended up in one of the main tents for more warmth. She determined that about 100 people slept in the main tent that night. Snow was a rarity in that area so there was a lot of talk about it. JaiJai was in charge of the wood stove that night. She remembered one woman who got upset because she did not think JaiJai was stocking it with enough wood. JaiJai explained it was a thin stove and too much wood would make it blow. It was a good thing JaiJai oversaw the wood stove that night and not that lady, right?

CHAPTER 26

Peaches, Huckleberry, and the Demon Girl

So, as the Rainbow Gathering died down JaiJai had to figure out a way to get home. Remember I said JaiJai met Peaches at the gathering? Peaches and his traveling companion Huckleberry, his dog, were traveling in a truck. JaiJai was trying to hitch a ride back to her rental house in Maricopa, Arizona and Peaches agreed to drive her there. He said he did not have anywhere else to go and so they traveled together to Maricopa and her house back in the real world. Peaches was NOT religious and absolutely did not believe in God. JaiJai, on the other hand, carried her bible with her everywhere she went. They quickly discovered this made a good talking point during their travels.

JaiJai had been gone for exactly a week when they arrived back at her rental. When they pulled in her driveway her landlord was standing in the neighbor's driveway talking to him. She flagged JaiJai down and said, "Oh good, you're back."

Evette said she needed to talk to JaiJai. She informed JaiJai she had gone bankrupt, and the bank was repossessing all her rentals. She shared with JaiJai that she had 30-60 days to move out. JaiJai said that she could spend those days looking for something else, but she had no ties there and realized there was nothing holding her there. Most everything she owned was already in her pack (except an air mattress). She had two t-shirts in the closet. She processed it and thought there was no reason to stay there.

Peaches was in the yard and was waiting to take a shower. She told him to come in and shower and explained that then they could decide where to go because she was leaving with him. She quickly gathered her things as she had decided she would head back to California with Peaches and Huckleberry. They took off. She had been planning to go back to her job and be an adult, but things quickly changed. "God has a plan," she said, "God has a plan."

They traveled together for almost a week. Their conversations kept coming back to God which she thought was interesting.

Street Kids: The Unloved, the Loved, the Lost, and the Lonely

Peaches and JaiJai went to San Diego to see a friend of his. When they arrived, they discovered that his friend had been shot and killed at a fast-food restaurant just days before. They ended up going to his funeral. Right after the friend's funeral JaiJai was struggling with a lot of life and felt she needed counseling or guidance of some sort. Long Beach California has a neighborhood that is nothing but churches. Catholic, Baptist, etc.… It was the middle of the week and Peaches went out with his friends while JaiJai went to the church neighborhood. She remembered she walked from church to church and each one she came to was locked.

Finally, one door was opened. There were secretaries inside. So, she went in and talked to one of the secretaries. It took the lady several minutes to acknowledge that JaiJai was even at the counter. Then a lady half-heartedly asked what she wanted. JaiJai said she needed to talk to someone, and the lady told her no, go on down the road. She turned and walked away feeling saddened, helpless, and somewhat hopeless. She said this happened several times as she walked into different buildings along the way.

She recalled thinking, "These were supposed to be churches." It was upsetting. After ten different churches and no one reaching out or being helpful, she walked into the last office she saw. There was a young man inside. He said he could not help her because it was not in his job description. He sent her to the Catholic church.

Walking down the road she met up with a priest and he handed her a pamphlet inviting her to church. She ended up sitting on the stairs of a building and talking with this young gentleman for an hour. Another homeless person came up and sat down. He shared the same thing that he had been sharing with JaiJai. This priest shared that his doors (Catholic church) are always open.

The day after JaiJai's visit with the priest, she and Peaches decided to travel north. JaiJai still carried her bible. Peaches still had a lot of religious questions. JaiJai chuckled as she said, "We sure made for odd traveling companions."

One afternoon, they stopped at a truck stop to get supplies. There was a girl walking back and forth, back and forth, again and again, in the parking lot. JaiJai recalled that she had crazy red hair. JaiJai and Peaches watched as the girl would start to walk toward a vehicle, get spooked and then quickly move away. They watched her for quite some time. Finally, JaiJai told Peaches that the girl obviously needed or wanted a ride but was too fearful to ask anyone. She decided that she would go over and offer the girl a ride. When she crossed the parking lot and got in front of the girl, she saw that her eyes were even more crazy than her hair. They were three unusual colors and both eyes looked different. JaiJai offered a ride. The girl said yes. She shared that she was headed toward Sacramento.

This was two hours north of where they were. Peaches and JaiJai agreed to head that way and take her.

JaiJai offered to let her use her phone card to call someone and let them know where she was. She called. It rang and rang. She said no one was going to answer, but she continued to let it ring. JaiJai finally asked her if she wanted to call someone else. Maybe her parents? The girl called again. She let it ring. She finally spoke aloud saying she knew they would not answer because her parents were Adam and Eve, and they were trying to deceive her [mind] into thinking she was their child, and she knew she was not their child because she knew that she was God.

"I know that I am God," she exclaimed. "In the year 1990 I got really angry, and that anger transformed me into a human figure, but Adam and Eve keep trying to convince me that I am their child."

JaiJai looked at her and listened to this crazy story she was spinning. When she paused, JaiJai asked, "If you're God and we all know God knows everything, then what is my middle name?"

She smiled and simply said, "Marie."

JaiJai said, "No, you are wrong. It is not Marie."

She said, "Oh, I'm not God! Well, thank you for explaining this to me."

This crazy red-headed, three colored eyes girl could quote scripture better than most people, but she would always put a twist on it. It was only a few minutes before she again began professing that she was God, and that Adam and Eve were trying to deceive her and convince her that she was their child. JaiJai listened and she highly believed she was demonic not only through her looks, but her words and her actions. While riding in the truck, Peaches' dog, Huckleberry suddenly tried to move between JaiJai and this girl. The girl simply turned her head, looked at the dog and laughed. The dog yelped loudly, suddenly jumped into the back seat, and crapped everywhere.

They could not get to Sacramento fast enough. As soon as they arrived Peaches gave her two choices. He said, "we will either take you to a church for an exorcism or to the police station, it's your call." At the next stop, the girl jumped out of the truck and took off running, leaving her belongings behind. Peaches and JaiJai just stared dumbfounded and then tried to figure out what to do with her belongings. Neither of them had ever witnessed something so bizarre.

They decided to drop her bags off at the Sacramento Police Department. They went in and told the police why they wanted to leave them. The police thought they were crazy when they told them what had happened. JaiJai said she was quite certain they thought both of them were tripping on drugs or something. They sat there for over two hours.

Finally, the police decided to go and look in the girl's bags. The police then came back to the room where Peaches and JaiJai were sitting and asked them where they were when she jumped out and what direction she was headed. They explained to them that she had been in an insane asylum for attempting to kill her parents and had escaped. It took all of that before the police would listen, but after searching her bags they believed them.

Peaches and JaiJai left and went and found a spot to camp for the night. The next morning, Peaches got up and the first words out of his mouth were, "Can we go to church?"

They drove that Sunday morning until they ended up in some random church parking lot. They went to church there. Peaches talked to this pastor about demons and heaven and hell for about an hour after the service was over. This pastor probably wondered what Peaches was on, but he was not on anything, he had just experienced a demonic girl.

Peaches and JaiJai camped that night. JaiJai recalled that she woke up on Monday morning at two a.m. and could hear Peaches crying. She listened for a moment, but finally asked him what the matter was. Peaches said he needed a hug. She asked him why and he said he was upset over everything that had been going on. She responded, "You know I don't cross those boundaries. She then asked him what had happened between the time they went to sleep and two A.M. He was quiet for a moment and then said, "If you won't give me a hug, then you're not my friend."

She said, "Fine, I'm not your friend."

He said, "If you're not my friend then you shouldn't be in my truck."

She said, "Then I'll get out of your truck, is that what you want?"

He said, "If you're not my friend."

She said, "Well, I'm not giving you a hug."

He said, "Well, you're not my friend."

"Not a problem," JaiJai replied. She got up, grabbed her belongings, her backpack and left. They were in Ukiah, California and she knew a few other people in the city. This was between Thanksgiving and Christmas. JaiJai ended up walking up to Tinkerbell and Brad's house because it was a safe house and because it was the closest place she knew. JaiJai recalled, "I knew I could go there and have a safe space without sleeping in a ditch."

CHAPTER 27

Brad and Tink

Let's talk about Brad and Tinkerbell and their safe house. JaiJai did not say how she knew them, just that she did, and they had a safe house for street kids near to where Peaches and her parted company. She smiled as she reflected on those days. "Brad and Tink would easily have 10-25 kids at their home on any given day. People would be lined up in sleeping bags on the floor."

Showing up at 2:30 in the morning was no big deal and she was welcomed with open arms. Ukiah, California has become a mecca for homeless people. According to the 2017 Annual Homeless Assessment Report (AHAR) to Congress, California's homeless rate has jumped 14 percent in 2016 - 2017 alone, identifying more than 134,000 people as homeless in that years' time. Prior to then, the homeless population grew nine percent over the previous seven years. Ukiah, California is no exception to the homeless population.

Just days after her arrival, Tinkerbell told JaiJai, "You need to go apply for government assistance…food stamps." JaiJai said, no, she would be fine without. Several days later, after seeing so many other homeless return with food stamps and/or groceries, she decided she would go apply. All she had to do was open a file, get photographed and fingerprinted. For JaiJai it was not that easy though and the assistance office finally told her to come back the next morning.

The next morning, she arrived early at the government office. They apologized for the difficulties, explaining that she already had a food stamp account in Eureka, California. However, there was no photograph or fingerprints on file. She told the woman she had never been to Eureka, California. The woman told her there was nothing she could do but give her access to that account. JaiJai walked out of that office on that day with a food stamp card with an approximate balance of $860.00 that needed to be spent before the following month. She decided to give back to Brad and Tink and bought their groceries for the coming holiday season, so that they could provide a nice holiday meal for the homeless that were staying in their home.

JaiJai sat on Brad and Tinkerbell's porch that afternoon with numerous street kids. Some were holding conversations, some were sitting silently, and many were playing with their best companion, their road dog. She said she remembered having some conversation with kids around her, observing the kids with their dogs and suddenly she spoke to the kid sitting next to her and said, "I want a dog." She immediately thought to herself, "where did that come from?" She had not realized she had been thinking about this, thinking how nice it would be to have a dog to travel with, to keep her company. The moment passed.

Another day passed. For some reason, she had not made any plans to move on, she was just spending time with those around her. Another morning on the porch with some of the same street kids and some new kids that had arrived throughout the night. The same street kid was sitting next to her when she made the comment about wanting a dog.

Hey, I live next door…" a Mexican man walked down the street toward them and said, "My buddy bought this dog and now he doesn't want her, so we'd sell her. Anyone want to buy a dog? $150.00". The boy sitting next to JaiJai smiled and said, "There ya go. Go buy yourself a dog."

This was when Viktorea came into the picture. The dog was in the backyard with a heavy log chain holding her there. She was a Boxer and American Bulldog. JaiJai smiled at the memory. "I knew immediately I had to save this dog."

It was obvious that the dog had been beefed up on steroids and prepped to be a fighter. Why they decided to get rid of her, she said she would never know, but she knew she had to take her no matter what. They agreed to give her the dog if she would give them $150.00 worth of Kool Aid, Cheetos, frozen pizzas, and a whole lot of other junk food. Upon delivery of the food, the guy cut the log chain off the tree and handed her the chain. It was still welded around her neck. *"That was okay,"* JaiJai explained. *"I didn't have a collar or anything because none of this was really planned."*

Shortly after taking possession of the dog, JaiJai said she began to feel uncomfortable with the situation and was concerned that they would come back for their dog. Just a few short hours later she decided it was time to go. From Ukiah to San Francisco she hitchhiked with her newfound companion, Vikki. She said she arrived at Golden Gate Park right at nightfall and pulled out her sleeping bag.

"I remember thinking...what in the world am I doing here? A strange dog, and another full moon in Golden Gate Park." Unsure of what to do with the dog, she shoved her down into her sleeping bag and climbed in. She smiled silently for a moment and then continued, *"I woke up in the night, stared up at the moon, looked down and realized the dog was right by my face, mouth open, yawning, staring up at*

me." JaiJai said she knew at that moment that everything was going to work out great with her new road dog.

CHAPTER 28

Occifer Viktorea Karmama

Their bond was amazing. Occifer Viktorea Karmama was the full name given to JaiJai's new dog. She called her Vikki and soon they were inseparable. She laughed as she said, *"I never really thought of having a dog, but after getting her, I couldn't imagine life without."* They traveled side-by-side and went everywhere together and nowhere alone. She reflected and said how interesting it was because she never felt fear on the road alone and was always independent. She said at no time did she feel the need to be protected, but that is exactly what Vikki did for her, whether needed or not.

She said that when she first got Vikki she had to figure out how to get the welded collar off of her neck and she hesitated to ever put a collar on her neck again because of its representation of bondage. Vikki had been kept in bondage. She had been pumped up on steroids and bulked up in preparation to be a fighter. She never knew why the guy chose to sell her that day. She did not know if he would be back for her, and she found herself constantly looking over her shoulder which is why she left the area as quickly as she did.

It was as if Vikki had been a part of her the whole time. She remembered fondly that their relationship was solid from day one and training was so easy or non-existent. Occifer Vikki just seemed to know when she was told to do something. JaiJai would walk her around the campsite telling her "Boundaries" as she did so. Then, she would set her loose and Vikki never left her boundaries but protected her lot.

Vikki loved to travel. She loved to hang out at campsites, and she loved JaiJai. She was loyal her entire life as if she were grateful for being set free from the chain of bondage. She loved to climb trees, to chase her tail, and to run freely through the tall grass. JaiJai was quick to learn of her loyalty to JaiJai on the streets. She witnessed firsthand Vikki's loyalty when she would come and sit next to JaiJai, between her and another person. Vikki was always calm, but she showed her authority when needed. She was respected on the streets amongst other street kids.

Chapter 29

So Many Travels, but No More Details

These stories could go on and on and I wish that I had followed God's word quicker, but I did not. Getting JaiJai to find the time, the energy, or the desire to open up about these past travels has become increasingly difficult. It was her past, her stories to tell. I take responsibility for her losing focus on sharing her stories because of dragging my feet these past 13 years. Maybe I used life as my excuse. In all honesty, I found myself hesitating, starting, and stopping because I was not sure of how or why this book was supposed to be written. I am human and I have struggled.

Michelle spoke to me in the beginning. I thought I felt her presence, her need to be heard. I know this sounds crazy to you the reader, but this is where it began. I heard about her story, and I put it aside. I went on about my life. I worked, I raised my family, but I spent many restless nights being tugged at, nudged, and finally pushed into the beginning stages of authoring this story. As I sit here proofreading, writing, and revising almost 13 years after the beginning nudges, I realize that those nudges came from God and that he had to be steering this journey. No one or nothing could keep me on this pathway for this long, with no end in sight.

Every time I tried to walk away, I found myself drawn back. **Romans 9:20** states, " Nay but, O man, who art thou that repliest against God? Shall the thing formed say to him that formed it, Why hast thou made me thus?" Who am I as a human to question what God has asked me to write? What gave me the right to hold back or to even hesitate in the sharing of these stories?

Michelle's story needs to be told. Street Kids need to be recognized. Of course, what I write about is only a small portion of a larger epidemic in our country that goes unnoticed or at least is minimized because it is not pretty to look at or it is such an epidemic that no one knows what to do to manage it. Our society needs to prioritize the health and mental well-being of those who travel and are homeless. Our government needs to recognize this, develop and implement a plan to better help those out there who have no one or other dysfunctions that need care.

Honestly, these last few weeks what keeps ringing in my head every time I think about sitting down to write is the fact that I know there are missing chapters. In fact, I have chapters dedicated to certain stories that are no longer mine to tell. I want to walk away, to give up, to scream, this is not my place to share these stories. Who am I to think I can write about Max, about Stonie, about numerous other people who have been brought into my research world so easily, step at a time? I want to tear up my pages, delete my work and yet I keep hearing Michelle through God say to me, "make it work, you have to make it work…it's time you finish this." Today, I found that end. My heart feels full of confidence and belief that it is time to put this story to rest.

These are not my words. These are stories told to me, molded by my pen to make you, the reader, understand the real struggles, heartache, mental breakdown of too many of our youth and young adults who have no one to rely on or to reach out to. It is necessary for you, the reader, to understand that the dynamics of those homeless street kids may differ from what our sheltered existence might have taught us. It is not just youth who ran away. Street kids come from numerous avenues to end up on the streets. Runaways, kicked out, lost, taken, not wanted, not loved, mentally unstable…all of these and many more reasons are what I have discovered in my journey of drafting this book. It has opened my eyes to this epidemic and I hope that it has opened yours.

Hopefully, someday I can add an addendum of chapters to this book that tells more stories of the street kids in San Francisco, about Taft who is homeless and, on the streets, Hopefully, I will be able to share about the not so safe house in Las Vegas. Maybe, I can share about JaiJai living in Quartzsite, Arizona in a cave or going to the Slabs again, to the Redwoods, her time in Los Angeles and so much more. Currently these are not my stories to share and yet God keeps nudging me to continue. How can I continue with these holes in time? Just like this, I guess…sharing with you the reader what I know, what I have discovered in research, by drafting the stories freely given, and through much thought and prayer. The other chapters must sit here for the time being, slots holding a place in time in hopes that someday they will be told. *Now, it is time to share with you the final several chapters that I must give to you, the reader.*

CHAPTER 30	**San Francisco**
CHAPTER 31	**Taft**
CHAPTER 32	**Barstow Snow**
CHAPTER 33	**Las Vegas…Not so Safe House**
CHAPTER 34	**Quartzite and Cave Living**
CHAPTER 35	**Slabs…Again and Again**
CHAPTER 36	**AlixAnne Beggar Dog**

Dr. S.R.G.Brush

CHAPTER 37   **North to the Redwoods…**
CHAPTER 38   **Los Angeles**

CHAPTER 39

Slabs and Brian David

Jai Jai's whereabouts was a mystery for the most part as she traveled all over and rarely called home. If you will recall in a previous chapter, it was shared that JaiJai's parents provided her with a cell phone. When she walked out of their house that day, she took that cell phone with her. Her parents never turned it off. She used it to call home on a rare occasion, but it was an exceedingly rare occasion. She liked her freedom, her independence. JaiJai did not want to be tied down or connected to her hometown. At some point JaiJai lost her cell phone and never replaced it. It was not important to her. Connections were not necessary in her world most days. However, one day something made her decide to call home. She borrowed a cell phone from a guy she had just recently met, Brian David. She said she could not really call him a friend as they had just met the day before.

JaiJai did not know why she decided that day to call, but she did, and she was completely caught off guard when she discovered one of her best childhood friends had recently passed away. She listened as her mom explained the details. She was in complete shock and tears as she said she would try to come home for the funeral but did not think she would be able to make it. JaiJai shared that she said her goodbyes and handed the phone back to the guy she borrowed it from. He saw her expression and knew something was wrong. He asked and she shared that one of her best friends had just died at the age of eighteen. She was deeply saddened and in shock. JaiJai told Brian David that she wished she could go back to Missouri for his funeral. Brian David said if he had a battery for his car, he would just drive her there himself and then he said goodbye and walked off. JaiJai went back to her campsite and pondered the situation, debating on walking off and hitchhiking home, stressing over the time constraints, money constraints and so much more.

JaiJai said that this next part is true and quite amazing. She assured me she was not making it up as she began to open up about her journey. She said, suddenly people that owed her money started showing up and paying her for the work she had done. She had cleaned for an older couple, and they stopped to pay her. She had run errands in town for another, and they stopped by her campsite and paid her, too. She said as she sat in amazement and looked down at the little over $100 she felt like God was trying to tell her something, but she was struggling to understand. Don't we all hit these snags in life? God speaks and we do not understand? God speaks and we question his plan? God speaks and we do our own thing anyway?

JaiJai sat at her campsite by her campfire mourning her friend's death, feeling helpless, and contemplating her choices. Soon, she looked up and Brian David was standing beside her. She was surprised to see him standing there, but even more surprised when he spoke.

"I was walking back over to my campsite, and I passed by an old friend of mine who called me over and told me he thought he had a battery from an old boat that would fit my car. He did and it does. I can drive you to Missouri tomorrow," He smiled down at her, and she hesitated. She had not known this man for even 24 hours. Why would she go in a vehicle with him across the country, she thought.

"We go as friends and nothing more," JaiJai stated firmly awaiting his reply. She knew he had acted like he liked her, and she was not interested in any of that. Silence.

"Okay," he replied, *"I will drive you to Missouri to your friend's funeral."*

The next morning, they took off in Brian David's old beat-up car. They were in Arizona and so they knew they had a lot of miles to cover. Their travels were going smoothly until they blew a tire. They did not have enough money for gas and the tire. They were stranded. As they were sitting there alongside the road trying to determine their next steps a vehicle drove up and a man told them to go to a certain garage and he would pay for their tire to be replaced.

They arrived at the station where the man told them to go. He paid for the tire and left. As the mechanic was replacing that tire, he realized that the other tire was about done for as well. JaiJai spent the rest of her money on that second tire, and they knew they were going to have to be creative to get home now because their gas money was gone. The tires were on and off they went, knowing that their time was limited. JaiJai told Brian David to go to the grocery store. He responded that this was not a great idea since their money was limited. She told him she understood, but to go anyway. JaiJai bought hotdogs and buns. Brian David looked at her questioningly. She walked to the corner and began selling them to the passersby. People would buy them and tell her to keep the change. Many drivers just rolled down their window and handed her money. The hotdogs were gone, and they had money to keep on going. *"God is good,"* she said. They traveled through the night. They spanged on the street corners when necessary to get the money they needed, and they finally arrived in her hometown the morning of the funeral.

JaiJai's mama said she remembered seeing her daughter pull up in the driveway with some strange man and all she could do was smile! Her daughter was home. She greeted both JaiJai and Brian David, ushered them into the house with open arms and felt her world was complete once again. Brian David was a big man with long dreads and a scruffy beard. He was kind and had a profound sense of humor. He seemed to fit perfectly into their home and yet no one asked JaiJai their relationship or how they came to be together. Brian David and JaiJai left for the funeral together. JaiJai's mom prayed they would return.

CHAPTER 40

Kegan...April 23, 2009

Kegan Floyd Hunt, 18, of Memphis, died April 23, 2009, in University of Missouri Hospital and Clinics, Columbia. Kegan was not a street kid. He never was and he knew nothing of the street kid life but had a tremendous impact on one specific street kid, and that was JaiJai. They were close friends. Their family was friends with her family. Kegan was a young man of good character, a strong Christian, and a caring friend. He spent a lot of time at JaiJai's house, hung out with her older brother, played around the neighborhood, and connected with her, as well. In fact, he spent enough time at her house that JaiJai always thought of Kegan as another brother.

JaiJai was on the streets when Kegan became ill. It all happened so suddenly one spring afternoon. Kegan came down sick and he was taken to the local hospital where they brushed his illness off as something viral and sent him home. His health deteriorated fast, and his family decided to take him to a bigger town several hours away where he was admitted. They were desperately trying to determine what was going on, but Kegan began to deteriorate quickly.

Not knowing Kegan had become ill, JaiJai's mom, Serena, was at home that afternoon and suddenly found herself super sleepy. She never slept in the afternoon but decided to head upstairs and lay down on her bed. It was the middle of the afternoon and she fell asleep almost immediately. She recalled how out of character it was for her to sleep during the day and she could not explain what happened or why she had laid down. When she woke up it was as if Kegan had come to her and had spoken very clearly to her and JaiJai's mom was at a loss as to what her dream meant.

"Tell my mom not to worry, I have the best seat in the house."

Just an hour later, his words were understood. The call came to let the family know that Kegan was in Columbia at the hospital and slipping fast. If anyone wanted to see him, they had better hurry. JaiJai's family was scattered, and her mom was the only one home to take that two-and-a-half-hour trek to the hospital and she did, fast. She had no way to contact JaiJai and even if she could, there was no time for JaiJai to return.

JaiJai's mom, Serena, entered the hospital room and stood silently, watching over the young man who was lifeless. His mother stood with tears running down her face. Words escaped them both.

Finally, Serena walked toward her, hugged her, and told her, *"I know this is going to sound crazy, but Kegan came to me in a dream and told me to tell you not to worry because he has the best seat in the house."* And they cried.

Kegan passed away later that night with his family surrounding him. Lemierre's Syndrome. Lemierre's Syndrome.According to: https://rarediseases.info.nih.gov/diseases/6882/lemierre-syndrome Lemierre syndrome is a rare, severe complication of bacterial infections. This syndrome does not prey on the ill, but usually affects previously healthy adolescents and young adults. It often starts with a bacterial throat infection, but then develops further involving the ears, salivary glands, sinuses and even teeth. It can also be in association with an Epstein-Barr infection. The primary bacteria responsible for infection in Lemierre syndrome is Fusobacterium necrophorum. However, other bacteria can be responsible as well.

Just days before the funeral, JaiJai happened to call home. She was nineteen and, on the streets, and that phone call gave her the devastating news that her eighteen-year-old friend had passed away. She was at a loss but said she would try to get home.

Lemierre starts out on the deep tissues within the neck but can quickly turn into septic thrombophlebitis or otherwise a clot filled with pus and infection that is in the internal jugular vein This clot circulates in the blood and the infection spreads quickly to the lungs and other part of the body causing respiratory distress and organ shutdown.

A horrible, horrible bacteria ridden disease that could have been cured had the hospital been more proactive. However, this disease is not common, so they overlooked it until it was too late. The heartache. The devastation. The loss. Another life taken way too early. A young man on the brink of his future, taken from the earth suddenly, leaving behind parents, brothers, a sister, grandparents, aunts, uncles, cousins, and friends. Another young person, never to be forgotten, one who made an impact on so many in eighteen short years.

Kegan's life was cut short. Kegan had found God and he had preached a sermon just a few days before falling ill and his desire would be to make a difference in this world. Looking back on the loss of this beloved friend, JaiJai realizes today that it was another piece of the puzzle, another step in life's journey, one that brought her home whether she wanted to be or not.

CHAPTER 41

Conversation About the Road

People talked. Of course they did. A small Midwestern town, what more did they have to do? JaiJai went to that funeral like any hippy would…barefoot, long skirt, and Brian David in tow. People looked. People whispered. Kegan's mom hugged her, held her, and they cried together. She did not judge her. She loved JaiJai like one of her own. They mourned together and yet celebrated together the life of Kegan. Finally, JaiJai came home. By that I mean that her mom was so happy to see her return after the funeral to her childhood home with Brian David. That night they ate, they talked, they shared stories of the road. Her family listened, asked questions, and was just so thankful she had returned. But for how long?

In all the conversations, JaiJai's mom and dad quickly realized she had no real idea who this Brian David was that they had invited into their home. In fact, she had known him less than five days. He seemed nice, but he did not share why he was on the road or for how long. Bits and pieces emerged, and they discovered that he was an ex-Mennonite from a broken family. This could take me, the author, down another rabbit hole (by now, you know, I am good at that). However, God tells me it is time to keep moving and get this story finished. Another time, another time.

Just a few days passed and JaiJai told her parents it was time for her and Brian David to go back out on the road. Her dad stood silently while her mother cried. Oh heck, she did not just cry, she wailed. She did not want to see her go. She wanted her at home. Selfish? Probably, but it hurts a mother's heart to see her own flesh and blood wander aimlessly around this crazy world. JaiJai was determined they should go. Brian David was just along for the ride…or was he?

That evening about 6 PM JaiJai's mother's phone rang. She answered. On the other end was the manager/owner of a campground site in Kansas. They told her to hold on and the next voice she heard was JaiJai. She was angry. She had been crying. Finally, she conveyed to her mother that she was at this campground, and they would not let her go. They had given her the option of calling her parents or calling the police. JaiJai chose her parents. Confused about it all, her parents agreed to drive the five hours and pick her up. She said she would be waiting. It did not sound like she had a choice, did it?

Her parents had no idea what had happened. When they asked where Brian David was, she said she would explain when they got there. Upon arrival, they found JaiJai sitting on a picnic table with the campsite owners nearby. She was ready to go and quick. Her parents thanked them and climbed back into the car to start the five-hour drive home.

JaiJai immediately launched into the fact that they were holding her there against her will. She and Brian David had gotten into an argument, and she decided she was not going to travel with him anymore. She jumped out of the car near the campground and started walking toward it. She needed to use their bathroom. While taking care of business, Brian David took care of business and told the owners that she was an underage minor and that they should call her parents. She stepped out of the bathroom to discover that they were giving her two options, and she was not crazy about either one. She had no identification on her to show that she was 19 years old. Her whole life she had looked very young, and these people believed her to be around 14. She was furious at Brian David but helpless as he had already jumped in his car and left the scene, leaving her to decide. She had to decide if she wanted to call the police or call her parents because these people would not believe the truth. Her parents drove her back home.

The interesting ending, if you call it that, to this chapter is that it did not end. By that I mean that JaiJai ended up staying with her parents for a year. She then moved out and into her own place, taking care of some elderly people, doing some cleaning, and odd jobs. This sounds like a great ending, doesn't it? The long-lost daughter was home. If only that were where the story ends.

Chapter 42

On the Road Again

JaiJai had been taking care of an elderly couple. It was a difficult job for her, but one she felt she was led to do. She watched as they grew frail, she passed, his dementia worsened and eventually he passed away, too. JaiJai was spent. She shared that this was something she felt led to do, it was rewarding and yet she did not want to continue to do this for others. She was not sure what her future held, but she believed it was time to travel again, and soon. One day she decided to buy a small camper and remodel it so that she could travel the roads in style. Her mother's heart sank, knowing this would start the roller coaster ride all over again. She remained silent though, knowing her daughter was an adult now and there was nothing she could do. She supported her. She loved her. She prayed for her.

Hours after hours of challenging work and her camper was finished, and she was looking forward to going out on the road again. An older friend of hers (in his late 60's), Ross, had helped her to redesign the camper, add new cabinets and flooring in black oak and a wood stove. She had moved chairs, made a bed, and designed as much storage as possible. Her camper was magnificent, and she felt very accomplished.

The morning JaiJai left on the road was the day when her mama's heart sank, and she felt ill. That afternoon JaiJai called her mom. Her camper had broken down in Kansas City. She was safe. She was in an auto part store parking lot. JaiJai explained she was going to work on it there and get it up and going. Days turned into a week. She tore her motor apart, trying to figure out the problem. Her uncle drove to Kansas City to try to help her determine the issue. Her friend Ross, who had helped her redesign the camper, drove up there, too. She ran into an old childhood friend on the streets while she was there and yet no one could figure out the obstacle that was preventing her from being on the road again. She was heartbroken. Her mom said she personally felt like her prayers had been answered.

JaiJai called the Ford garage, and they towed it to their lot. She waited and waited. Finally, the news came. The motor was blown. There was no fixing it. She decided to pack a duffel bag and take off walking. As she was packing, she realized she had three dogs and a cat, and this herd would make traveling on foot too difficult. JaiJai called Ross again and asked him if he would come back to Kansas City and help her get her belongings. She told him he could take the wood back out of the camper if he liked, but that she was donating it to an organization that helped the homeless have places to live. The camper would be set up as a makeshift home for someone. Ross arrived that afternoon and helped her load most of her belongings in his car and they headed toward home.

JaiJai was frustrated that her travel plans were stopped…no, delayed. She knew she wanted to go out on the road again and be free from structure, rules, and such. This was a setback only in her mind. She would travel again. Even if it meant going home, reorganizing, and taking off on foot. JaiJai was sharing with Ross that her plan was just delayed. She was going to take off from home hitchhiking once she got home, reorganized everything, and left the cat. JaiJai's plan was to be on the road again in just another day or two.

They had not gone far when Ross pointed out a school bus for sale. She told him she wished she could afford it, but she dropped all her money into the camper. They turned around and went back to look at it. Ross told her he would buy the bus for her, and she could pay him back. He shared with me, the author, that he felt it was the best decision because at least she would be leaving and traveling with her own transportation and not hitchhiking across the country and getting in with God knows who. Ross bought the bus and he drove it home with JaiJai following in his car. They parked the bus at Ross's home and JaiJai quickly shared with the family what her plan was. Ross and JaiJai were going to gut the bus out and start all over designing a vehicle for her to travel in. In the meantime, she opted to live on her bus at Ross's house. The rollercoaster ride continued for all involved, and the hills and valleys were steep.

CHAPTER 43...

Do You Believe in God?

This question should have been asked in the beginning. A good friend of mine used to always tell me that you do not go at something head-on, but you go through the back door so that you do not create drama or tension but slide into it making everyone involved comfortable. So, let us just say that is what I am doing here. I have mentioned God numerous times. I have shared with you the tugging on my heart to write this story. I mentioned the fact that I could not find information for a long time about Michelle Thorndike and then it appeared and later it disappeared. I reminded you numerous times that God has played a part in this entire process and that if it were not for Him, this story would not be told. So, obviously, you know my belief in God. I hope you can tell that my belief is strong. It is and as I type this, I want to share my amazement at how He played such a strong part in so much of this and made certain that I saw those moves He made throughout.

JaiJai's story is God filled. In hearing it, I believe JaiJai had a plan, a desire, a want, but God had different plans, and this was difficult for JaiJai to accept. She wanted her will, not His. JaiJai worked on her bus gutting it out, but also picked up some jobs to help pay for her expenses. Her process was moving, but slowly. She quickly realized the bus was going to keep her stationery much longer than she had anticipated.

Between work, bus, and friends, JaiJai spent time with her family as well. Her mother was planning a day trip to another state to take care of many errands she had to do. JaiJai decided to go too because she wanted to pick up her medical records from a doctor's office in that town. Her uncle Ken asked her to go too because he had a meeting that same day in the town where they were headed and did not have a ride. They all three decided to go together. This was the first time they would travel together and the last.

JaiJai's mom showed up at Ross's with Ken, but JaiJai was not ready. In fact, she seemed stressed. She still needed to make coffee, she said. JaiJai's mom decided to get her vehicle's oil checked at a local station to give JaiJai time to get her coffee. While at the station getting their oil checked, Ken decided to move from the front passenger seat to the back seat. The station put a little oil in because it was low and then made an appointment for the following day to change the oil for her. They headed back down to Ross's. JaiJai was outside waiting. Immediately she was stressed that she had to get into the front seat.

As they drove off, she said, "I thought I would sit in the back,"

Her Uncle Ken said, "I can move up there if you want."

Her mom said, "I can pull over at the cemetery for you to switch seats."

JaiJai said no. She was fidgety and obviously anxious. Finally, her mom asked her what was wrong. She said she did not know. She was having a tremendous amount of anxiety about going on the trip and even more anxiety about riding in the front. Again, JaiJai's mom offered to pull over, but she declined.

Approximately eight miles later, life changed. "Oh my..." her mom screamed and then they hit. The backhoe turned directly in their path, impact was hard, and then she watched as the backhoe drove off. Suddenly smoke appeared as she heard her brother Ken in the backseat calling her name repetitively. She turned and screamed that they had to get out, the vehicle was on fire. JaiJai was gone. She looked out the window and about a football field away she saw the backhoe going down the road and near that she saw JaiJai running down the middle of the road and then... collapsed. JaiJai's mom turned to get out of the car to run to her and as soon as she turned, she said, "Damn." Ken was in the back asking if she was okay, what was wrong. She said harshly, "Nothing is wrong. Are you okay?" Ken said his back hurt, his back hurt, he thought he had broken his back. She started to cry as she realized she could not get out because her right leg was about four inches shorter than it should be. Her foot was crushed. Her daughter was lying in the middle of the road and her brother on his back in the back of the van. The rest was a blur.

JaiJai's face was broken in numerous places. Ken's back was fractured and JaiJai's mom's ankle was shattered. JaiJai's plans to travel were put on the shelf for the unforeseeable future.

For now, for this book, I will leave JaiJai's story here. Her present and her future are hers to tell. Why I share with you what I share is because it is evident that God's will is done and not our own. We may have plans and aspirations, but God has the ultimate plan. We need to silence ourselves and just listen. He is the commander of our journey if we will only allow it.

Also, I want to point out that there is such a diversity in street kids. I know I have said this before, but I believe it important enough to say it again. What makes one come home while another stays out on the streets and yet another dies from jumping off a train? What keeps one clear minded, while one is daily in a drunken stupor, another drugged up, and another with mental health issues. Who designs their journey?

CHAPTER 44

Michelle Rachel Thorndike... Revisited

Why me? What do I hope to accomplish in authoring this book? Such a loaded question with a lot that I have pondered over the years as I have struggled with the calling to author this book. As I sit in a school classroom and look out amongst the students, I wonder what their future holds? Who will succeed? Who will struggle? Who will flounder? Where will they end up? Do Michelle's teachers remember her? What did her education look like? Could she have been saved?

She MUST be remembered. Michelle Rachel Thorndike (A.K.A. Max), born March 3, 1990, passed away June 15, 2008. Her life needs to make a difference. She has made a difference in her brother Sam, I believe.

If you have read this far, you have taken a tremendous amount of information in and may have forgotten who Sam is in relation to it all and how we made our connection. Michelle Thorndike's brother, Samuel Thorndike and I met via a simple little thing called technology. I sent the following message (this is where I repeat myself to you):

Hello. I'm not sure where to start with this, so bear with me as I try to explain WHY I am writing to you. My name is Samantha and I and 52 year old mother of four. Many years ago, I heard a story about a girl named Michelle Rachelle Thorndike and her sad death in 2008. This story was told to me by one of my friend's daughters. I said at that time that I needed to write a book about street kids and specifically focus on Michelle. Why? I don't know. It was a feeling. I started that book. I think that was in 2011... however, life got in the way with family, education, work, and eventually a car accident. Life has really been put on hold for awhile. Anyway, the last few weeks, I have fallen asleep and Michelle...a.k.a. Max as called on the streets has been weighing heavy on my mind. I've been waking up with her in my first thoughts of the day. I don't know why and really cannot explain it. I am hoping you are her brother and I am not just rambling to a stranger. In trying to research, I understand that Michelle's mother (and pos-

sibly yours if I'm right on who you are) passed away before Michelle. I am so sorry to hear this. Please, if you are Michelle's brother, I would love to learn more about her and her life and anything you can and are willing to share. In return, I will tell you the story I know, which isn't much, only if you want to know. Thank you in advance for your patience reading this and please, let me know if you are indeed the Samuel Thorndike I am looking for. Thank you.

If you are, I want to also say how sorry I am for your losses. My family has had a tremendous share of loss as well, starting with my brother when I was nine and my mother when I was 12 years old, so I do understand. I've lost another brother since, along with other family members. Life is short, Michelle's was shorter and I feel there's a story there that might make an impact on someone's life. Thank you.

He responded. It was that day that I realized that the only thing stopping me now from writing this book was me. God had nudged me repeatedly. JaiJai had shared some amazing stories, my research of Michelle was starting to develop and now there's Sam.

I am not sure how I would react if someone were to contact me about my brother who passed away and his not so perfect past. Well, honestly, I THINK I know how I would react, and it would not be as open, honest, or as sincere as Sam has been with me. This guy really has it together and wants the world to know his sister, to remember her, to learn from her. He wants the memory of Michelle "Max" Thorndike to make a difference, and so do I.

CHAPTER 45

Tell me more, Sam

Sam left home when he was fifteen years old because his father's new girlfriend did not want kids around because hers were grown and already moved on. Sam admits he was rebellious. He ended up stealing a bottle of alcohol from a grocery store and got caught. He was put into a juvenile youth detention center because of his age, and they would only release him to his parents' custody. His mom had long since passed away, and his dad did not want him, so he sat there for six months until he turned sixteen. At sixteen they released him on his own recognizance which meant he was released… to the streets.

Sam shared that he mostly lived with friends and some family after he was released from the facility. He spent some periods of time sleeping outside and camping. He did whatever he could for money, but it was never a real job. Eventually, he found himself caught up in selling heroin to support his own growing habit. He spoke about his habit, and how he found himself working to get clean with the support of many of his friends. He accredits these friends in his journey to recovery and his ability to stay clean.

As time passed, he became a father to a baby boy. It is obvious this child means the world to him. He went to court to get fifty percent custody. He named his son after his mother, to keep her memory alive. His relationship with his father is rocky, to say the least, and they are rarely in contact. Sam shares that he now is the proud father of a daughter, too. He accredits having kids to giving him a vastly different outlook on parenting and realizes that his father's treatment not just of Michelle, but of himself too, was so incredibly wrong. At points in his life, he shared, he felt like he had no place in the world. In those days, he often thought if he died, no one would care.

I asked Sam, "What would you want to share about your life that I might not have asked? Anything?" His response was, "I think what happened to my sister really sucks. She had no chance to grow into herself, she got to experience a lot of the bad without much of the good. I'm really thankful I was able to turn it around and experience all the good life has to offer, and I like to think my sister and mom live on through that in me and my kids."

I have never met Sam, but his story and his life make me proud. Proud to see an individual who came through much and learned that life is about the choices you make. Sam chose to get clean. Sam chose to take responsibility. Sam works a real job. Sam learned a beautiful trade, making jewelry, and although we never met, I purchased a beautifully unique ring from him that I wear daily. As a mother, I feel I can say confidently that he has made his mother proud.

CHAPTER 46

Reaching out to Horsshit

As the author, reaching out to Horsshit was not a straightforward process in many ways. First, find him. I looked and looked but did not know his real name and could not seem to find any connections for several years. Then came the police report! Yes. A name. Well, okay...maybe three possible names. It was a start. It always seemed like when I got added information on this story that I would shut down for a bit. Sometimes it was a day and other times it was weeks. This time...a couple of weeks went by where I felt immobilized...frozen…. uncertain of my next move. Then one morning I woke up and it was as if I knew and it was not me making the decision, either. I know how crazy that sounds. Try being me and living it. I woke up, grabbed my coffee, slipped in front of my computer and BHAM...sent without hesitation...to one contact...then another...and another. Finally, a fourth one suddenly caught my eye. The name was different and did not fit the names found in the reports, but something drew me to it. What the heck, I thought as I copied my original message:

Good Morning. My name is Samantha. I am writing to you on a difficult subject and definitely do not want to stir up any hurt or heartache and am afraid I might. I am hoping 13 years has helped ease this request. If you do not want to talk with me, please just let me know. If you are willing, that would be great as well. I wish no ill will. So, I came across some information about a girl named Michelle Thorndike and have learned a little of her home life, her life on the streets, and her death. It's almost as if her story has haunted me for several years and I feel the need to write about her and other street kids. For several years, I have avoided this, but it continues to come back to me repeatedly, and this summer I decided I need to give it my best attempt. I understand that you were her fiancée and went through heartbreak and devastation with the loss of her. Would you be willing to share any information of your life with her, of her death, of your life on the streets, anything? I see that you are recently married. Congratulations! Also, what beautiful talent you have with what appear to be palm leaves, right? Thank you, in advance, for your consideration.

Why had I not done that weeks ago, I thought as I turned off the computer, grabbed my tennis shoes and stopped by the kitchen to drop off my coffee cup before heading out back to the flowerbed. PING. I heard my phone in my back pocket just as I began to work on the flowerbed. PING. Oh, could it be a response from him already? I thought about this as I stood silently by the flowerbed, wondering if I was ready for this door to open. Ready or not, here I go, I thought. I fished my phone out of my back pocket, turned it on and saw the icon displaying I had one unread message. Deep breath in. Deep breath out. It was not him. Disappointment.

I finished what I was doing outside, and I remember how hot it was that day. I went inside, took a shower, and got dressed to go to a baby shower about an hour away. The shower was fun. It was one of my past students who had invited me and had recently given birth to twins. Twin boys. I sat and watched as the family gathered, so many kids played together, and everyone enjoyed meeting and holding those new baby boys.

My mind wandered down a rabbit hole a little bit as I sat there taking it all in. We are all born so innocent. Some of us are born into better families than others; some of us have better upbringings than others. We all have choices we must make. How do we get the knowledge to make the best choices? How will those two little boys turn out? They are twins, they could grow up doing the same thing together or they could choose to make quite different choices and end up completely different in the end. Choices...my phone went PING. I pulled my thoughts away from that rabbit hole and stared at my phone. Another unread message. Not going to get my hopes up, I thought, as I turned back and tuned into the baby shower happening before me. It was a nice shower, with great people, but my mind would not settle, and I found myself peaking at the message below:

> Horsshit sent June 19 at 2:08 PM
> *Wow....u freaking rock... yeah Max is what she went by...she was soo f#@king rad...i truly miss her very very much...she was only 18 and it's really sad that she died on june 14 2008 in amarillo texas somewhere around 3 a.m. give or take... we traveled hard....and loved one another very much so.it broke my heart and it never healed...sometimes i wish i was dead...and i would always take her place if i could...so sad ....*

I am not going to lie. My heart raced as I read and reread his message. It was him! I found him. He was okay with my reaching out, even excited at the idea of my writing this book. My emotions were in overdrive and my mind was whirling so fast that it was difficult to know what to say and I knew I could not focus and write while at the baby shower.

PING. Another message as I read the first message for the third or fourth time in just a matter of four minutes.

> Horsshit sent June 19 at 2:12 PM
> *I keep her alive everyday and i always think about my frog...it's what i called her my lizard girl, or frog girl...lol*

They unwrapped the "twins" ball, revealed the gender and opened presents. Oh so fun, and yet I was anxious to depart and to write back to him. I snuck a quick message into him between activities:

> You sent June 19 at 2:48 PM
> *I'll message you when I leave an event in a few hours. Thanks*

He responded with a simple okay. That was it. I finally have connected. A portal had opened, and I had so many questions. I was so excited at the prospect of learning more. We finished showering those babies with love and I headed on my way, saying a quick prayer that their lives turn out well. Right before I began the lengthy drive home, I sent a message:

So, I would love to know more about how you met, where you traveled, life on the road...

Life is a journey and I am thankful to see that you have moved on and found someone. I am interested and hearing more about your life if you are interested in sharing. I have heard that you 2 were truly in love then and good for each other.

He responded with "In a sec" and I said, "NP." Now for the drive...and the wait. Jesse randomly sent me a picture of a dog, his dog I assume, sitting in a kiddie pool. I responded with a "sweet" comment and told him I was in Missouri, and it was an extremely hot day here. I waited. What a weird feeling of uncertainty.

Horsshit sent June 19 at 6:36 PM
Currently not married.... but Max was my world i would die for her..we use to always get arrested together....yeah,she was the most amazing ,and she had a smile that lit up the back of the police car i can tell u that much...every day i think about her

Jesse changed the chat theme to Kiwi.

Horsshit sent June 19 at 6:42 PM
We were a team from hell,especially when copa were involved....lol

> **Horsshit sent June 19 at 6:42 PM**
> Cops
>
> **Horsshit sent June 19 at 6:42 PM**
> And when we were as we would call it then,"RAGING IT" ...cops were like a everyday thing...
>
> **Horsshit sent June 19 at 6:42 PM**
> i loved her,still LOVE her...never will stop loving her...im sad
>
> **Horsshit sent June 19 at 6:42 PM**
> Talk to me

I read his comments to me and my heart hurt. It hurt as if it were a fresh wound all over again. He still hurts. He was still mourning her, still in love with her all these years later. I pondered where to go with this...I did not want to bring up painful memories, but I longed to know more.

> You sent June 19 at 7:07 PM
> *How did you meet?*
> *I'm so sorry if I'm bringing up old hurts .*
> *I thought I read you were recently married. Sorry.*
> *What is, "raging it?"*

> You sent June 19 at 8:17 PM
> *Would you be willing to share about your childhood? How did you end up on the streets? Are you still on the streets?*
>
> Horsshit sent June 19 at 8:18 PM
> oh yes...im going to share my entire life story just for u...just to u....
>
> **Horsshit sent June 19 at 8:18 PM**
> I trust u...

If you know me, you know I can be very sarcastic at times. I read and reread his comment that he had trust in me, and I could not wrap my mind around it except to think that he was being sarcastic. I mean, how can a complete stranger receive a message from a complete stranger and instantly say yes, I will share my entire life story for you...I trust you? I knew I had to respond but was unsure of how to word it.

> You sent June 19 at 8:21 PM
> *I am humbled if this is true (and not sarcastic). I will tell you I am a mother of four grown children, all very different, a high school teacher, a person who desires to write.*

While I waited for his response, I was unsure of what to expect. I found myself shaking my head at the idea that I had started this journey several years back and how everything was happening in its own time and without me making many decisions. I truly felt that I was being driven by a higher power. Now there I sat in communication with the man who once was a boy in love with a girl whom I had never met but feel totally connected to. How crazy do I sound? A girl who lost her life jumping trains, a girl who endured too much in her short lifetime and died too young. He responded:

> **Horsshit sent June 19 at 8:22 PM**
> im being soo honest with u

> **Horsshit sent June 19 at 8:22 PM**
> I love that

I told him that was awesome for lack of better words. He instantly wrote back and said:

> Horsshit sent June 19 at 8:23 PM
> Im different.u never met someone like me ever

I asked him why that was and then went on to tell him that I had met some street kids before, thinking he thought maybe I had never met anyone like that. He told me to look at his story. I told him to please share. He told me to watch his story. I asked him where it was. I told him I had learned a lot about Max through research. He said it was his Facebook story. I then messaged him:

I want to hear why kids end up on the street. Is it by choice or no choice? Michelle was forced out from what I have learned.

His response came quickly:
Horssshit sent June 19 at 8:33 PM
call me

You sent June 19 at 8:33 PM
Can I call you Monday at some time?

Horsshit sent June 19 at 8:36 PM
U should xae while i have the chamce im a very busy persom amd right now im able to talk

Horsshit sent June 19 at 8:36 PM
I am not ur everyday average train kid...i am the Horshit....Max knew it... amd u wilk know it i will sgare my emrire story iif u call me right mow..

Horsshit sent June 19 at 8:36 PM
I will tell u what hapoened amd how it happemed the real true story that no one knows

You sent June 19 at 8:43 PM
Video Chat
6 mins

Yes, I reached out and called him. I remember the call well as in my physical location, but the call itself was a whirlwind. I was collecting eggs from our chicken coop; he was telling me he had been greenlighted after her death. I asked what that meant, but he continued. He said it got so bad at one point that he had to fake his own death. He told me how heartbroken he was and how he would never heal from the loss of his lizard girl.

His phone almost died, and he had to run across the street to plug it in. He shared that he no longer drank and that yes, he was on the streets. I asked him if we could set up a time to talk later as I had other commitments and he agreed. We decided we would talk in two days. I hung up with a sense of urgency from him, and a feeling that I should have spoken longer.

That night he messaged me:

Dr. S.R.G.Brush

Horsshit sent June 19 at 9:05 PM
OK I JUST GOT BLOCKED BY SOMEONE CLAIMING TO WALK WITH GOD...LOL

Horsshit sent June 19 at 9:05 PM
HYPOCRITES

Horsshit sent June 19 at 9:05 PM
THANK U FOR NOT JUDGING ME

Horsshit sent June 19 at 9:05 PM
EVERYONE SEEMS TO HATE ME FOR NOTHING
You sent June 19 at 9:05 PM
No judgment. I look forward to talking to you.

You sent June 19 at 9:06 PM
Take care.

My heart aches. I cannot explain it. This poor, lost soul. It is obvious he is a mess. I sat and calculated his age and was shocked to think that he must be close to 35 years old now. He was still on the streets. Nothing in his life has changed for the better. He is living day-by-day and has nothing. Why? What were his choices? I have no hatred for him, just heartache for a person who seems so lost, so alone, and no understanding on my part as to what has happened to him in his life except for the loss of a loved one that was on the streets with him...the loss of his lizard girl, Max.

Another message:

Horsshit sent June 20 at 12:55 AM
FOR ALL THESE YEARS I'VE BEEN ALONE WITH MY MEMORY OF MY TRUE LOVE,AND IT'S SO GOOD TO FINALLY MEET SOMEONE ELSE OUT THERE THAT REMEMBERS HER....I LOVE AND MISS HER SOO F#@KING MUCH...

The next night another message rolls in:
Horsshit sent June 21 at 12:44 AM
TOMMOROW IS THE BIG DAY..I'VE BEEN WAITING TO TELL THE TRUTH AND LET THE WORLD KNOW ABOUT HOW EVERYTHING HAD WENT DOWN JUST AS IT HAD WENT DOWN ....MAX IS MOST DEF.STILL ALIVE AND EVERYDAY THAT GOES BY I ONLY LOVE HER MORE AND MORE...I KNOW THAT SHE LOVES ME AND IS WITH ME AT ALL TIMES... AND ONE DAY WE WILL BE TOGETHER AGAIN BUT IN A DIFFERENT MUCH

Dr. S.R.G.Brush

MORE HOLY AND RIGHTEOUS PLACE IN HEAVEN WHERE SHE WENT

I woke up and read his message and responded:
>You sent June 21 at 7:13 AM
>*I look forward to hearing from you.*

This was the day we planned to talk face to face. He kept putting me off...one more sec...one more sec... I cannot imagine what is going on in his world, so I wait patiently. I do not know where he is, what he is doing or anything else...so I wait.

Life happens and sometimes gets in the way. Sometimes it is easy to put this topic on hold. It is so emotionally tolling on me at times and can draw me in fully and make me feel like I am drowning in it all. I do not want to make this about me though, so I want to address the fact that it also MUST be tolling on Stonie, on Sam, on all who have been asked to revisit the death of Michelle.

CHAPTER 47

Horsshit's Childhood

Do you ever look at someone on the street and ponder their beginnings? Do you wonder where they came from? How did they end up on the streets? What brought them to the place where you see them today? How do they appear? Are they clean? Neat and tidy? Organized and well supported? Dirty? Disheveled and lost? What exactly do you see? Did you even stop to look at them at all or did you just quickly walk on by with your head dropped down so as not to notice? Be honest, if not with me at least with yourself. What is your perspective on homelessness in America? What do you know? What about the "Street Kids" on our streets? Are you educated about them? What are your thoughts? You do not have to tell me or anyone else, but I implore you to think about this group of citizens who often go unnoticed or are labeled negatively no matter their situations.

I do. I always have…thought about them, that is. I cannot explain why. It might have had something to do with my childhood and the hitchhikers that my father brought home. Maybe it was my own child who chose to live on the streets. It might have been because I met JaiJai. It could be because of the couple I saw begging for money to buy food for their child. Then there was the older guy I saw begging on the Las Vegas strip near our hotel room. The one I watched at the end of the day, went around the corner, and hopped in his Corvette. I am sure that the small group I invited in for Thanksgiving dinner and how they celebrated with music but chose to live so poorly with a debit card of cash available at all times had an impact on me. So many visuals, each so different. It all makes me realize that these people are just like any others, trying to survive in this crazy world, the best way they know how…by the choices they make…and their choices bring them to their place in this world.

Let us talk about Horsshit and his beginnings. As anyone who thinks about those on the streets like I do, I have pondered questions of, "What? Why? When? How?" What brought him to the streets? Why is he living on the streets? When did he come to the streets and when will he go? So many questions that whirl through my mind, but these are the beginning, which is appropriate, I guess, because this is the beginning of my friendship with Jesse…a.k.a. Stonie…a.k.a. Horsshit.

Not long after I met him, we had our initial six-minute conversation while I was in my backyard collecting chicken eggs. I chuckled at the thought because it was an extremely sweltering day, I had my head half in and half out of a chicken coop and my phone was sitting on the edge looking up. That conversation was choppy to say the least. Stonie asked me what I was doing and when I told him I was collecting chicken eggs, he was quick to say they have fresh eggs…sometimes. I do recall pieces of our conversation, but oh, how I wish I were able to record it and listen to it…again and again. I feel I missed a lot, and it is information I might not get back. We agreed to chat again, but that did not seem to be coming to fruition at this point. Finally, I decided that I had to ask Stonie in a message:

You sent June 21 at 9:37 AM
What brought you to the streets originally when you were younger? Are you still on the streets?

I was not sure I was ready for his answer. Our lack of connection face-to-face was partially my fault, too. I really was struggling with how this situation should go. What should our conversations look like? What should I ask him to dredge up without seeming selfish on my part? Was I going to hear things that would make me uncomfortable? Again, so many questions. Well, I decided to go with the beginnings...because that is where all people's lives start.

His answer came quickly:

Horsshit sent June 21 at 9:45 AM
Well it has to be said like this, i was adopted at five years old by my aunt and my uncle both named xxx xxx xxx and xxx xxx xxx...well supposedly to get me out of a f#@ked up family and for other crazy reasons. Anyway what they were supposedly taking me away from inevitably happened anyway when i turned 16 and my dad(also my uncle) had took it upon himself to molest me, and he called it some kind of "FAMILY TRADITION"..and that fucked me up pretty dang good. So then i just lived with it and the moment i turned 17 i was then sent off to a private teenage juvenile prison, the second worse in the state of Louisiana and waited til i turned 18 then was released...then i went to Florida met my real parents for the first time since i was five, didn't get along with them...actually turned out to hate them just as much.so i started to hitchhike from Florida all the way to California. Right as i get to San Diego my bag had been stolen...welcome to Cali right?....that's a little bit of what first got me onto the streets. There is much more to the story and how it unfolded and i end up being who i was and who i still am today...

Horsshit sent June 21 at 9:46 AM
It's most def true i'm tellng u now that it's for real and it's legit

You sent June 21 at 9:47 AM
I totally believe you. What a horrifying start. I am very interested in visiting more with you. Tell me when you 1st met Max? If you don't mind?

Wow, I did not waste any time, did I? In looking back over our messages, I wish I would have taken more time to reflect and think about where to go next. I jumped too quickly from his brief description of his childhood to how he first met Max. I was afraid I would lose him, that he would vanish without me learning more. As I reread his words, and I do quite frequently, my heart aches for a young boy who is lost. Lost to what? Lack of a solid childhood? Poor parenting? A poor system that failed him?

CHAPTER 48

Meeting and Spending Time with Max

I wish I had met Max. It is a strange world to know that a 52-year-old woman is sitting at her computer desk in Missouri writing about an 18-year-old girl from Rockport, Maine who lost her life in a train accident in Amarillo, Texas. A girl she never met. A girl who only crossed her path due to a story that was told to her by a girl who met this girl Max's boyfriend, Horsshit, on a Greyhound bus in South Dakota. They only met because so many people were standoffish to him, the bus kept breaking down and she befriended him. Ironically, she came from Montana and was headed to Northeast Missouri, and he had started in Amarillo, Texas and was trying desperately to get back. A little mishap in Kansas City and they find themselves thrown together and train hopping to Amarillo, but I am getting a little ahead of myself. Let us go back…to the carefree meeting of Horsshit and Max…a.k.a. Michelle Rachel Thorndike. Let us hear Horsshit's account of their meeting.

You sent June 21 at 9:47 AM
I totally believe you. What a horrifying start. I am very interested in visiting more with you. Tell me when you 1st met Max? If you don't mind?

Horsshit sent June 21 at 9:50 AM
I first met my Lizard Gurl in Ocala,Florida,at the national rainbow gathering….she was at the camp they called the OnUrWayCafe….and i threw a burning log with my bare hands at her boyfriend at the time and told him to kick rocks that she was my girlfriend now and she thought that was awesome and we left the scene.

Horsshit sent June 21 at 9:52 AM
I was pretty dang hardcore at this time,and still nobody messed with me at all. She knew that she was 100 percent safe with me…and i always took care of her..and she really enjoyed the 99 cent ice creams at the McDonalds…sometimes it would have to be her ice cream over my tall cans of steel reserve malt liquor,but anything for that gurl….

You sent June 21 at 9:54 AM

That's awesome. I can truly tell that you loved her. Can you share with me some of your adventures?

Horsshit sent June 21 at 9:56 AM
Yeah, we started out hitchhiking on the interstate once we took off from the gathering in Ocala...and i taught her how to easily freak the cops out and stop them from searching us by putting an open condom with mayo in it in our outer pockets and they would find it and be so disgusted that the search simply ended

You sent June 21 at 9:57 AM
Lol! How creative!

Horsshit sent June 21 at 9:58 AM
We stuck our thumbs out the entire beginnig and didn't hop trains quite yet until we reached El Paso Texas...but i would hide somewhere in the bushes and have her stand there with her thumb out while wearing some smaller size pants and some dudes would pull over and i would be the first to tell them that we were heading the same direction and to give both of us a ride....it worked flawlessly

You sent June 21 at 9:59 AM
How long were you two together?

Horsshit sent June 21 at 10:02 AM

We were together for a good year i think...not nearly long enough...we used to RAGE like crazy...and we were always finding ourselves in the back of police cars all handcuffed...lol

Horsshit sent June 21 at 10:02 AM
We traveled a really long adventure before the night of june 14th 2008

Horsshit sent June 21 at 10:02 AM
i used to carry this really huge bowie knife and when we hitchhike people thought twice about f#@king with her...

Was it love? Was it acceptance? What do you think? I think in talking with Horsshit and reading his words that he saw he met, he conquered, and he completely fell in love with his Lizard Gurl, his Max...Michelle. Someone who loved him back, someone who he could take care of and protect from the world. You see, I had heard Horsshit had a heart, JaiJai told me. She said she witnessed it on the bus that day and in their travels together. Then I met and talked with him myself. Underneath that "street kid" exterior is a loving, compassionate, protective individual who lives day in and day out in agony because the one person he fell in love with who loved him back unconditionally, he could not protect. He could not save her, and he did not know this until weeks later. I read what he wrote, and I felt his love, I felt his pain...I felt his desire to tell of his time with Max, a story he held to himself, a story he was eager to share. A story I was eager to hear... adventures I wanted to know.

You sent June 21 at 10:02 AM
How did you get out of situations like that?
Please share that adventure as well, if you will.
If you need to take a break, let me know.

Horsshit sent June 21 at 10:03 AM
She was all innocent like and really kind and also very very ditzy like, but i thought that was the greatest

Horsshit sent June 21 at 10:03 AM
Im good...we can keep going

You sent June 21 at 10:03 AM
We can talk face to face later to day, or this evening, if you have time.

Horsshit sent June 21 at 10:03 AM
I always have the time for Max.

Still, even today, it is obvious that Horsshit's love was real. Genuine. I shared with very few people about my journey into this book and what I saw as my courageous leap into conversation with Horsshit, but I did choose to share with one specific friend and her immediate reaction was, "he did it." She said, "You are just a small-town girl. I do not think you would recognize a psychopath or someone who may have committed a drug-induced crime." Her words hurt briefly. I get frustrated at how quick people are to make judgments and try to break people down. I do not think this was intentional on her part, but it is what I felt. I closed the conversation rather quickly.

Horsshit, if you read this...I believe in you. You had a sucky life from the beginning, and you grew up and ran at first chance. You searched for stability in parents that were "unavailable" during your childhood only to discover that they were just as bad as those who raised you. Unless something more comes out in my research and our conversations, this is where I stand. You, too, have been a victim. Yes, I think you have made choices, and I do not necessarily agree with ALL choices, but that is between you and God. Who am I to judge?

I will continue to pray that you decide to sober up someday and leave the drugs behind. You admitted to me that you are an addict, and this is more heartache added to the story. Think of the sequel that we could have. The boy, turned man, who lost his love chooses to rehabilitate and live life healthier. I do not know. No one can make you; it is all about your choices.

You sent June 21 at 10:04 AM
What is your favorite memory of your time together?

Horsshit sent June 21 at 10:08 AM
I think i had lots of fave memories...but this one time we were in Texas doing our thing in the bushes and the police walked up on us...told us to just put our clothes on and leave..lol

Horsshit sent June 21 at 10:08 AM
That was in Bridge City Texas

Horsshit sent June 21 at 10:08 AM
It wasn't the only time that happened either..lol

You sent June 21 at 10:09 AM
How did you two end up travelling by train?

Horsshit sent June 21 at 10:09 AM
We were stranded in El Paso TX and we heard trains in the distance and got puck

You sent June 21 at 10:10 AM
What does puck mean?

Horsshit sent June 21 at 10:10 AM
Picked up by the cops who dropped us off by the west-bound train tracks....that was our first hop ever

Horsshit sent June 21 at 10:10 AM
Picked

You sent June 21 at 10:13 AM

Street Kids: The Unloved, the Loved, the Lost, and the Lonely

What was your scariest time on the streets before or with Max?

Horsshit sent June 21 at 10:14 AM
really not many cuz i was just so fearless

Before meeting Horsshit, I believed that hopping trains was a norm for Horsshit and Max. I was surprised to learn that it had not been and that in fact it was something new to both. For some reason, this made more sense to me. I would like to know more about their train hopping experiences, however, Horssshit's conversation jumped from their first hop ever to how he felt immediately after learning of the loss of Max. I did not want to stop his flow of conversation and so I chose to go with it, to read what he wrote, knowing I might have to come back to parts of that conversation at a later date. Horsshit went down his own rabbit hole, opening up to me about his life after the loss of Max.

We have all lost loved ones in our lives, haven't we? Very few people are innocent of the heartache of death and loss. It is a season of life or seasons...but, imagine having no one in your corner for so long and finally meeting that one true, unconditional love only to lose her suddenly with no advanced warning, no one there to support you or care for you when you find out.

Horsshit sent June 21 at 10:15 AM

Time went on and months after the thing went down,i was in really bad shape over it...then every one hopping trains started accusing me of her rape and murder that really hurt me very badly

You sent June 21 at 10:16 AM
Where were you when she passed? Can you tell me how it went down?

Horsshit sent June 21 at 10:16 AM
But time went on and i healed slowly but not completely., Still to this day im hurting for her..i miss the hell out of her very very much.

You sent June 21 at 10:17 AM
Were you with her?

You sent June 21 at 10:17 AM
I have lost loved ones, so I completely understand.

Horsshit sent June 21 at 10:18 AM
We were in Amarillo Texas, just got out of jail was in for a whole week and the day we were released was straight magical...we met some train taggers people that sprayed trains with paint cans and they dropped us off in the train yard.

You sent June 21 at 10:28 AM
Please do not hesitate to let me know if I am overloading you with all the questions.

You sent June 21 at 10:28 AM
I know it's probably hard to think about some of this.

Horsshit sent June 21 at 10:32 AM
But before they dropped us off we stopped at the gas station bought a bunch of forty ounce beers and the alcoholic drinks with the caffeine called juice and we bought a bunch of crack from some dude in the front selling rocks then off to the tracks....sat there for a whole [day] drinking getting f#@ked up together,then the train rolled south bound and stopped..i was really messed up on alcohol and been smoking a good amount of crack with her and we got on to the grainer perch and sat on the train and waited

Horsshit sent June 21 at 10:34 AM
Ur good. i can talk about it nowadays just for keeping her alive sake

Horsshit sent June 21 at 10:34 AM
It's important that she isn't forgotten so i always tell her story when i can

Horsshit sent June 21 at 10:34 AM
My Frog Gurll...lol/Lizard Queen/life mate

You sent June 21 at 10:36 AM
Do you remember what you and Max had spent that week in jail for?

You sent June 21 at 11:13 AM

Hey, I am going to be away from my phone for a while. Feel free to write when you can and I will get back to you. Take care. Talk to you soon.

Horsshit sent June 21 at 12:39 PM

We went to jail for soliciting on the freeway off ramp...holding signs spanging for money and were doing good too..she would fly the sign all pretty while i sat under the bridge drinking and the cops showed up then had her in cuffs so i said f#@kit ran down there and picked up the sign then started to hold it again so i would go to jail with her...we both got arrested,then did a week and the entire time in the jail i was able to yell and communicate with her thru the hallway it made all the inmates pissed off but nobody told me anything except the cops that ran the jail....it was pretty fun...but that night on our release date,she got killed on accident by an oncoming freight train

Horsshit sent June 21 at 12:42 PM

It was such an awesome time being with her those moments that we shared until the very end.then it was sad and heartbreak when i ended up in Vaughn, New Mexico way outside of Amarillo...then made my way to North Dakota and then to Texas at different meetup spots all in the matter of one week... didn't find her...i was torn the f#@k up.

Stonie's story matched up almost exactly to the other stories that were shared with me of Michelle's death. Pushing to learn more was difficult and I hated to continue, but felt I had to try again.

I'm so sorry. When and how did you learn of her passing...? You were separated? How did you end up in those places? Too many questions?

> Horssshit sent June 21 at 12:49 PM
> *i did a lot of hopping north and south and had some crazy run ins with friends we had met in other states ...almost killed myself too*

> You sent June 21 at 12:49 PM
> *Oh?*

> You sent June 21 at 12:50 PM
> *Did you separate on purpose?*

> Horsshit sent June 21 at 12:52 PM
> *No the bulls were scanning the area where we had all the beer bottles and tagged the walls and using their spotlights trying to find me but i layed on another train rolling west bound that's where i ended up*

> You sent June 21 at 12:53 PM
> *Oh... so you ended up on separate trains?*

Horsshit sent June 21 at 12:54 PM
that was right when she died and i didnt know it happened just yet

You sent June 21 at 12:54 PM
Oh man, when did you find out?

Horsshit sent June 21 at 12:55 PM
A week or so later

You sent June 21 at 12:55 PM
How?

Horsshit sent June 21 at 12:58 PM
Same cops that arrested us the week before...they saw me making a call on the payphone to the taggers asking them if they saw Max

You sent June 21 at 1:00 PM
Oh wow. Devastating. Did they just come out and tell you? What did you do? I can't imagine.

You sent June 21 at 1:00 PM
You had friends... taggers for support, I hope?

You sent June 21 at 2:19 PM
I read somewhere that Michelle lost her mom when she was 13. I feel a connection with her. I lost my mom when I was 12. My family was dysfunctional, too.

Horsshit sent June 21 at 2:48 PM

Street Kids: The Unloved, the Loved, the Lost, and the Lonely

I PRETTY MUCH HAD NO FRIENDS THIS WHOLE TIME

You sent June 21 at 2:49 PM
What did you do? Where did you go? Are you still on the streets?

Horsshit sent June 21 at 2:50 PM
YEAH,IVE BEEN ON THE STREET MY WHOLE ENTIRE LIFE PRETTY MUCH

You sent June 21 at 2:53 PM
Was Michelle broken? Lost? Doing what she loved? I have so many thoughts and questions.

Horsshit sent June 21 at 2:54 PM
SHE WAS SOO HAPPY WE JUST WANTED NOTHING BUT EACH OTHER ALONG WITH PARTY FAVORD MOSTLY ALCOHOL ,SOME DRUGS NOT SO MUCH FOR HER..SHE LOVED HER ICE CREAM CONES..SHE WAS SOMEWHAT VEGAN TOO THO

You sent June 21 at 2:55 PM
I often wonder why people's lives turn out like they do…. circumstances and choices.

Horsshit sent June 21 at 2:56 PM
CHOICES,RISKS

You sent June 21 at 2:57 PM
I have heard you were soulmates. I've heard you were so good to her...a protector. I've also heard people accused you of bad things. So, you mentioned being green lighted? What does that mean?

Horsshit sent June 21 at 2:58 PM
ITS ALL SUPPOSED TO HAPPEN I BELIEVE... LIKE DESTINY LIKE...IM SPIRITUAL AND SOMETOMES I WALK AMONGST THE DEAD, AND ITS PRETTY INTENSE TO FEEL THE SOULS THERE WITH U...

We ended the conversation at this point because he was not with me anymore. He was somewhere else, wherever his drugs took him. My heart hurt. My mind swirled, but I knew there would be another day, at least I hoped there would be.

CHAPTER 49

My Thoughts on Matthew

I wish I could tell you this chapter was going to be chalked full of information, full of the details of Matthew Thorndike's life. I know he is Sam and Michelle Thorndike's brother. I know he, too, experienced a lot of pain, suffering, and hardship in his childhood. I do not, however, know his personal story fully. I did find Matt, and I reached out to him. He did respond. I wrote:

Hi Matt! Sam said he thinks he mentioned me to you but was not sure. My name is Samantha. I am drafting a book about street kids, with a focus on the memory of your sister, Michelle. It is a long story as to how I started down this path, but I have tried to sidestep it many times and swear I feel your sister pushing me to tell this story. In fact, someone who NEVER knew her, told me the story of her death and that is how it began. So, here I am. I reached out to Sam, and we talked. I have visited with several others. I would love to talk with you about your childhood, your memories, your lifestyle, and anything else that might be relevant. I am not typically available on the weekends but thought I would at least try to connect with you to see if you are interested in talking with me. Sam says you have a better memory than him. LOL. Thanks for considering this. Just let me know.

Matt's Response:

"Ya pull up"

I was quite pleased to see his response the next day when I opened my laptop. He was willing to talk. I had another person to pull information from and details to fill in the blanks or so I thought. I quickly typed some questions:

Awesome. I was hoping you could give me your recollection of your childhood. Share with me about your early years, your mom, when things went down (fell apart) and how you ended up on the streets.

Did you and Michelle stay connected?

How did you learn of her death?

Are you close/connected with your family today?

I have lots of questions. Please let me know if I overload you. That is not my desire. I want to get as many perspectives as I can.

Matt's Response:
Well I'm not rlly on the streets now but I do alot of drugs so I feel stuck in that sense I was angry at my dad for a long time but kinda got over it

I pondered a bit before responding. The questions were swirling so fast in my brain I could hardly organize them. I am talking with Matt, brother of Sam and Michelle. The kid on the streets, the missing piece to this family dynamic. Okay, questions:

Oh okay. I thought you were [on the street] sorry. Do you work? May I ask personal questions about your drug use? You say you are stuck in that sense…do you want to quit? Did you start because of your mom's death and the dad problems, or did you use before?

How long were you on the street?

Do you have an apartment?

I have written approximately 80 pages about Michelle and street kids.

I have met her fiancé (via messenger). He was so in love with her and still mourns her. I want her to be remembered.

This time Matt was quick to reply. Technology is great, but sometimes you must be patient. I hate the wait.

Matt's Response:

I don't have a job rn and ya I do wanna stop using but I'm not rlly sure how to like go forward or whatever I started using because I thought that it was cool to be different and that it would make me feel different I do have an apartment.

I was only 9; when my mom died so I def didn't start using bc of that but I think that if she hadn't died I might not have been drawn to that sort of life as much as I was

I thought for a bit and then I wrote:
May I ask how you pay for it? Your apartment... What drug do you use? Are you an addict? 8 years old? Wow. I am so sorry; I did not realize you were that young.

Were you all kicked out into the streets or moved out on your own?

When I am writing do you want me to change your name or use your real name? Sam said I could use his real name....

Have you always stayed in Maine, or have you traveled?

Do you have any religious beliefs?

Nothing. Ghosted. Those questions were all posed over two years ago. Wow, time goes fast. I waited, I hoped, I never heard. I finally decided yesterday that I needed to complete or delete this chapter and I was leaning toward deleting it. I mean, who am I to disrupt someone's life, especially all these years later. I sent him another message but had determined I would not write a chapter on Matt without more information from him. I wrote:

Hi Matt. I hope you are well. I'm not sure if you remember me, but I wrote a couple of years ago because I was writing a book about Michelle's death and Street Kids. I asked some questions. I am trying to finish this book, delete what I cannot get (information wise). I was hoping you would answer some of the questions for me. Are you interested?

I had a free moment during my work day and so I opened my book on my computer, found this chapter and had just deleted a line or two when suddenly I saw my phone ringing. I reached over and picked it up, it was Matt. WHAT? He was calling me? I quickly declined the call and messaged him, *"I'm at work. Sorry."*

All good. How do you know about my sister?

A street kid told me. I have done a tremendous amount of research. I have the police report, I have talked to Sam. I have talked to your dad (not sure he was keen on my writing this…). I would love to have more information from you and anyone else…

But I have promised myself I will finish this soon. It has been too long. I am 85% finished. I have talked to her fiancé.
Did you know there is a song?
Can you talk around 3:30 Central time?

No I didn't know the song and ya thatd be fine.

We had a plan. We would talk and talk we did. Matt was incredibly open and forthcoming. I felt our conversation, like every other journey in this book, happened when it should and provided added information in the time that it was needed. It is crazy, really. When I look back on the journey of this book and how pieces of the puzzle continue to appear all along the way, showing up only when needed.

The first thing I recognized during our initial call was the intelligence level of Matt. His conversation though sprinkled with some slang and a few curse words from time to time, was chalked full of a strong vocabulary and a highly intelligent thought process. Matt shared with me the fact that he originally had a lot of animosity toward his dad, but over the years he came to terms with their situation and came to realize that their dad was just a man, a regular person who was trying to get through life with what knowledge and experience he had. He definitely did not have "raising the children" knowledge or experience and when his mom died, his dad tried to step in, but did not have the skills necessary to manage three children. His father, a captain of a sea boat, was a bully-type man, meaning someone who barked orders and expected you to follow through NOW and not hesitate.

Matt shared that there was controversy in the household and that his dad struggled with raising the kids. There were arguments, battles, dysfunctions, and such but now he realizes that his dad was just doing whatever he knew how. Matt also shared with me, sprinkled in the middle of everything, the fact that his parents got married, but never planned to have kids. Sylvia had her first child at 30 years old. So, both parents were somewhat older than the typical parents of this time.

When Matt was twelve years old, he and his father had a big argument. His dad accused him of stealing a bottle (which he admits he did) and Matt said he got so mad, he ended up just walking out of the home. After a while he ended up in trouble and was put in a youth center for teens. They called his father to get him, but his dad said he did not want him back. Matt believes today that this was his dad's way of trying, "tough love." Matt ended up in the youth center awaiting placement. He ended up being placed temporarily in Sand House which was a holdover shelter for kids until another placement could be found. At some point he was placed in Oliver Place in Bath, Maine. Oliver Place is a place designed to be one of the most innovative providers of youth residential, mental, and behavioral health services.

Right before he turned sixteen, he was released back to his father who was now living in Florida. Matt went to his dad's home, stayed for a month, and realized he could not do it. He stated twice that there was nothing specifically wrong, nor did anything really happen. He just realized staying at his dad's house was not for him.

Matt moved back to Main and lived with his grandma, his father's mother, for a little while and then ended up moving from place to place staying with whomever would let him, but also drinking a lot of alcohol during this time. He paused in his conversation and then stated, "I was a sophomore."

Soon after these events, Matt found himself signed in to Phoenix House in Augusta, Maine. Phoenix House was a wild ride, according to Matt. It was a drug rehabilitation center, but Matt's view of it was much different. He shared that Phoenix House shut down and it did not surprise him with all that was happening around there. Matt shared that he met a girl while at Phoenix House and when released, he went to live with her in Portland Oregon. They were able to get a house through a teen center and all was good. Or was it?

They were together for three years before breaking up. Matt finally admitted to me that this girl was his ticket to opiates and Percocet and they were, "just having fun." It was not serious at this time, but soon, he turned to heroin.

Matt and his girlfriend broke up and he decided to take off in a car full of kids he knew to California. At some point along the way, there was some conflict, so Matt and his boy Will decided to get out of the car in Portland Oregon. They began walking and hitchhiking and finally made it to San Francisco where they stayed for a couple of months. Matt decided he wanted to go home so he went to a local General Assistance Office and requested a bus ticket home. Things like this always amaze me because I had no idea programs like this existed, so I wonder how others know. Anyway, he received a ticket and headed back home.

When I asked Matt about his living conditions, he offered up that he currently lived in an apartment and that his girlfriend takes care of him. By that I mean she provides daily to his drug habit, by providing his drug of choice, heroin. Let that sink in for a moment. He does not work. He is 28 years old. He shoots up daily and has for ten years. His girlfriend, "takes care of him."

I wish I had asked at what cost? What expense is this to her? At what cost is it to him (physically and mentally) to shoot up daily? Our conversation was great, he seemed very clear minded and forthcoming. I did not want to push too far. I did ask him what it was like to be addicted and for so long. He shared that there was a 2.5-year stint that he was on subs [substitutes] and off heroin, but it did not last. Previously in the text I had asked him if he wanted to quit, but he never answered. On this call he shared with me the difficulties he faced with the idea of quitting.

"My whole life is encircled by it, if I didn't use it, I wouldn't know what to do when you stop. That's when the difficult shit happens." Matt paused.

"Not wanting to get sick…you know….life after heroin is scarier than shit, too. You have to deal with everything that you previously have been able to ignore because you're high everyday."

I did not want to burn him out on questions, so I decided it was time to change them up a bit and redirect our conversation to Michelle [Max]. I asked Matthew what he remembered most about Michelle because he was quite young when they separated. I know he thought about this, as there was just a brief silence and then he spoke:

"Michelle was older than me. Because of this, we were not close. We didn't go to school together, but I will tell you Michelle was a badass. Smart as fuck! I don't know if this is true or if I made it up in my head, but I am fairly certain Michelle spoke French and could write it, too. Michelle kept a diary in French, I'm pretty sure. So no one could read it."

Matt stumbled a little over his words…." I believe she went to England with her class, overseas when she was 15 or 16 years old. She always wanted to travel. When she had her mind set on something she knew what she was doing. She was not your typical street kid. She wanted to live; she did not leave with the intention of dying just three months after turning 18. Michelle could have walked in off the street at any time, and I am confident she could run a fortune 500 business successfully."

Michelle's worldly events of her childhood affected her much more than it did Matt because she was older and much more aware of what was going on in the family dynamics. She internalized this. She internalized the traumas of her childhood. I [the author] relate to this more than I want to admit. Michelle's demeanor changed according to Matt. "She became a different person after her mom died. She presented herself as a different character to the world and often came across as off putting to a person. She turned to Punk Rock, she began cutting herself, we grew up rural and she wanted to see the world." Matt went on to explain that Michelle's final introduction to the street came when her dad told her she needed to tame down her hair or something like that to get a part-time job and help out at home. Their dad was not happy with her Punk Rock appearance and when he strongly suggested this change, she refused and walked out the door.

Matt's love and admiration of his sister echoes the same as the love Sam shared previously about Michelle. I recognize this brotherly love and I understand it because

I grew up with three brothers of my own. I hope Max knew of this love.

I asked Matt about his future and any dreams he has at this time. He thought that was a really deep question, but even that did not leave him speechless for long. He said he hoped to get enough good points in his life, to have enough clout spiritually to be remembered.

ADDENDA: The day after my friendly conversation with Matt, I received a message from him that read as follows:

But ya u have been thinking about it since we talked and I know that the dude she was w killed her and I think it is naive of u to listen to/believe anything he has to say and to give him a platform to rewrite history is wrong and disrespectful to the memory of my sis she was a person who could have done anything and some junkie idiot hobo killed her for no good reason I don't doubt that ur intent is pure but you are being conned and with all that said at this point I can't be party to what your doing do plz don't write anything about me other than that I think whavur doing us abhorrent and disrespect of an immense magnitude to my family

I sat in total silence for a moment, reading and re-reading the words sent to me by Matt, trying to get a grip on the gist of it and what his expectations are. It sounded to me as if he did not want any part of the interview, the book, or the situation. Finally, I wrote back:

Oh wow. I am shocked at this. Heartbroken really. I am not naive at all but have done a tremendous amount of research. If I had any doubt, I would be the first to tell you. I have talked to many people.

I feel like you have done a complete turnaround. I am not sure why.

Trust me when I tell you that Michelle wants me to write this book…either Michelle or God is guiding.

I will change your name and make you a fictional character if necessary.

I was in hopes of illuminating Michelle in her life.

Matt responded: *Like it jus doesn't make sense to me if he jumped off how was he completely gone before she dud like obv it was within 30 sec of him jumping and why would he go so far away and get them further separated idk um not trying to offend u but I have spent the entire time since she has been gone being told that he killed her and ir the only person who seems to think other wise I appreciate u trying to tell her story.*

And another thing is she called my dad pretty soon before it happened like within a month and wanted to come home but hadn't get her or bit ticket obv so idk I believe that she was prolly in love or whatever but clearly they were both unstable and impulsive ppl so it does not seem so far fetched that he push her off whe. They fighting and spend the rest of his life wracked w guilt over it.

He believed, like many others in the beginning, that Horsshit was responsible for the death of Michelle. He had heard...he believed. He did not want to consider otherwise. He had walked away from all the good stuff I had written thus far and was requesting I not include him. Darn, I thought. That chapter was finished. It was time to move on. What do I do now, I wondered. I sat and stared at my phone, unsure of my next move. I did not want to delete this chapter again. I had already done that once when Matt had ghosted me in the beginning. In fact, I was deleting this chapter when he called. I sent another message in hopes he would change his mind:

Originally, I was told this about her death as well. Through my research I have determined, and the police determined he was innocent. I am sorry this is hard for you.

If you do not want to be a part of this book, please let me know you stand by your words to not include you. I will change your name and move forward. I am saddened but will accept this if it is what you want. I believe this book will happen non-fiction or fiction. My desire was to share about Michelle's life and death. I can fictionalize it if I must.

In less than an hour, I had one last message from Matt:

I think ur doing what ur doing for the right reasons and you can write about me and use my name the only thing I ask is that u say that I think that the guy did it.

Relief flooded over me that I had not hit a brick wall and was not stuck in the chapter of Matt. I responded:

Okay, I can include your opinion. I have a person who deals with cold cases in Texas who has agreed to investigate her case. So far everyone that I have talked to about this case believes he is innocent.

So, for you the reader, I share these messages so that you can get a better grasp on what is being said, how Matt is reacting, and to hold up my promise and let you know that Matt believes that Stonie killed his sister. This is a grudge he has held onto for many years. It might be difficult to let it go.

CHAPTER 50

Summing it All Up

Where to go from here and what to say...I would be lying to you, the reader, if I told you I felt confident that I was ready to sum it all up. If you read this far, and I sure hope you did, this chapter is where I want to talk about...street kids, again. I know...I know...the whole book has been focused on street kids, so what is the difference, you might wonder. Well, nothing really, except that it is my hope to tie it all together for you. We have discussed numerous street kids and their stories. Horsshit and Matthew are still on the streets living their street kid lives...even as adults. JaiJai and Sam moved beyond the streets and are living settled in their community as single parents, raising the next generation, and praying to do better. Then there's Michelle...Michele Rachel Thorndike... Max... gone, but not forgotten.

Street Kids: The Unloved, the Loved, the Lost, and the Lonely

This whole journey started when I heard a story about a girl named Max who lost her life by train hopping. This story was told to me by a girl named JaiJai who met a boy named Horsshit while traveling on a Greyhound bus. All of them come from different walks of life, choosing to live on the streets or having that choice made for them. All of them have made choices. My choice is to end here, but it is a difficult choice as I feel like there is so much more to be said. Stories to be told, pains to share. The voices of these individuals are all but silent.

She tapped into my dreams again. I woke up in a sweat. It was so vivid, so real. It had been a while and was truly unexpected. She looked haggard, scared, almost desperate. "Don't let me be forgotten," she begged as she tugged on my shoulder. "Don't give up on me like the rest of the world did" she cried. "You must tell my story...the story of street kids. If not for me, for my brother, for others who wander like I did." She faded away quickly as I lay there in the dark realizing that once again Michelle was calling out to me. I know how crazy it sounds. I really do.

You see, I told myself this book would be completed before I started back to school in August of this year (2021). I tried, I really did, but life got in the way and before I knew it, I was back in the classroom, doing extra-curricular activities, and only dreaming of finishing this book...someday. Michelle is persistent though. She has a story to be told, a life not to be forgotten.

Overall, this story is about two girls, Max and JaiJai who never met, but an impact was made. It is about a boy named Horsshit, about the world and how small it can be or how messed up it is. I would like to think it is about explaining street kids, about giving "kudos" to Samuel who pulled himself together, about a brother named Matthew who is still out there struggling. Matthew, your sister wants you to change for the better. Our world today is in desperate need of better mental health care for those on the streets. This book is about so much that it is hard to narrow it down even here as this book comes to an end.

Horsshit lives. He is still on the streets. Kegain passed, but he lives on in the hearts of many. A boy named Richard, young and only God knows if he is still alive or not. Max, a.k.a., Michelle Thorndike and JaiJai….one lost her life tragically and yet her story impacted JaiJai so tremendously that her journey ended up off the streets and going another route. These stories were shared to show the complexity of lives in our world today, the street kids who all come from various levels of society and how some do not make it, others thrive, and others stay stagnant in their everyday world.

Chapter 51

Coming to an End

There is no better way to end this book than the way it began. You might wonder what I mean by that, so let me explain. I started the book with a minimal obituary about a girl who I thought was unknown, had no one and was going to be forgotten.

Imagine my surprise and happiness when throughout this process I discovered she did in fact have family, and as I was writing my last paragraph or so I thought, I was introduced to…Michelle's friend, Breezy. Before I could even reach out to her, she reached out to me. She wanted to know who I was and why I was writing about her friend, Michelle. Michelle was like the sister she never had. Sam and Matt were like family. She, even after all these years, held tightly to that relationship and it was clear she loved Michelle. She never knew Max. It was Michelle she spent all her free time with. It was Michelle whose heart she related to. It was Michelle, she mourned. She still mourns. She shared her memories, her heartache, and then she shared with me that Sarah, another friend of Michelle's and Breezy were truly heartbroken that there was so little written about the life of their friend.

A year after the loss of their friend Breezy and Sarah published a memorial in their local paper. I never came across it online and found it amazing that it came to me as I began wrapping up the closing chapter of the story that has tugged at my heart for years. A perfect ending to a not so perfect story, a sign that she was genuinely loved by many, and she will never be forgotten. Her life did make a difference.

That loving memorial read:

In Loving Memory of:
MICHELLE RACHEL THORNDIKE
March 3, 1990 - June 15, 2008
"The Girl Who Laughed in the Face of Danger."
A whole year has sped by since the day we lost you. We know you're up there laughing at every time we mess up, and praising us when we do something constructive.
And most of all we know you've finally found
peace and are once again with your Mom.
We can't wait for the time to come that
you're finally able to tell us about your adventures you had while living your dream.

> We miss you, love you, and we know you're always with us. Til we meet again, your friends,
> Breezy & Sarah

My heart is full. Some of her story has been told. It started with nothing, and it grew, and it built one thing upon another. From a girl unknown, the story of Horsshit [Stonie] and Max [Michelle], her sudden death, his heartbreak, her family, and finally her friends I have discovered the story of a girl who was broken, but also of a girl who had a dream and no fear of chasing that dream. A street kid who went places and did things. Obviously, her time before Horsshit will never be known, but it is certain her confidence in living her life on the edge took her places and now it is time for her to rest. Thank you to the street kids who have shared your stories either directly to me or through others. Thank you JaiJai, Stonie, Jordan, Clark, Sam, Matt, and Breezy for all you have shared. Most of all, thank you Michelle for your persistence in keeping me on this journey from beginning to end, sharing your story and that of the many street kids who often go unnoticed.

EDITOR'S NOTE: In authoring this book, I wanted you, the reader, to not only meet and remember Michelle and other street kids, but also to gain knowledge about the street kids that often go unnoticed in our society today. I hope you enjoyed the journey I have taken you on and now it is with comfort and confidence within my heart that this long journey is ready to close, and I can finally say, "The End…for now." ~Dr. S. Brush, 2024

Author Bio:

Dr. S.R.G.Brush, a prolific writer and accomplished scholar, began her writing journey at the tender age of five. Since then, she has penned numerous short stories and poems, earning the Tom Arnold Scholarship for Writing in 1993. An esteemed academic, Brush holds a B.A.Ed. in English, an M.S.Ed. in ESOL, and an Ed.D. in Educational Leadership from Saint Louis University. Living in the Midwest, Brush and her husband raised four children and have one grandchild. Brush relishes her time as an educator and enjoys family, the outdoors, travel, and her pets. With a belief in divine guidance, she brings a unique perspective to the crisis of homelessness in *Street Kids*.

Milton Keynes UK
Ingram Content Group UK Ltd.
UKHW022131051124
450708UK00016B/1279